belief in the broad social good from families achieving home-ownership led him to become one of the country's leading FHA and VA lenders. His business success also derives from planning ahead, knowing that a down market today could be up tomorrow, and that a booming market today won't last.

—ED DEMARCO
President, Housing Policy Council
Former FHFA Director

Any historical reference to the United States mortgage market, especially the last twenty years, must include Stan Middleman and the significant expansion of Freedom Mortgage into an industry leader. Stan's vision, exceptional work ethic, and inability to take no for an answer made him an industry titan whose advice and counsel are in high demand.

—BRIAN MONTGOMERY
Partner, Gate House Strategies, LLC

Success is never an accident. It takes commitment, drive, energy, risk taking, and the keen sense to go a different direction from the herd at times. I first met Stan when I was FHA commissioner at HUD back in 2010. In the years since, I've seen how Stan has turned Freedom into the massively successful institution it is today while remaining basically a family-owned company. Freedom, under Stan's leadership, remains on the forefront of the success stories in the mortgage banking industry. Over the past many years, Stan has shown his insights that separate him from others. From bold moves to grow his servicing portfolio, technology implementations that have reduced friction in his loan operations and servicing to significant moves in channel focus on the origination side of the business. This book is a must read for all current mortgage executives as well as the up-and-comers who want to understand what it takes to be simply better than the rest.

—DAVID STEVENS, CMB
Former FHA Commissioner

This book is a joy. It is both the story of Stan Middleman, the founder of Freedom Mortgage, one of the largest government lenders in the country, and a look at principles for managing a successful business, merged together into a really enjoyable to read book.

—LAURIE GOODMAN
Urban Institute

Stan is not a "go with the flow" guy, and his somewhat unorthodox approach has served him well as he has created and grown one of the nation's largest mortgage lenders and servicers. He has a passion for providing homeownership opportunities to people from all walks of life, and he gives back generously to causes and organizations that strengthen our communities.

—ROBERT D. BROEKSMIT, CMB
President and CEO, Mortgage Bankers Association

Stan Middleman possesses all of the qualities and then some of the most successful among us: talent, drive, perseverance, and imagination. But what most distinguishes Stan is his heart for the mission—the mission of giving every Main Street American the freedom to choose to own their own home.

—KURT POTENHAUER
Vice Chairman, First American

Seeing Around Corners is an insightful story about a mortgage banking icon, Stan Middleman, founder and CEO of Freedom Mortgage. As a Pennsylvania native, hearing about Stan's early years in Philadelphia and his serial approach to entrepreneurship from a very early age helps us understand his journey to leading a top national residential mortgage originator and loan servicer. His story is not for the faint of heart yet shows young entrepreneurs not to be afraid of failure. The book showcases Stan's indomitable character and his values as a leader. By *Seeing Around Corners*, Stan anticipated the mortgage cycles over three decades and achieved enduring success as a result.

—FAITH SCHWARTZ
CEO and Founder, Housing Finance Strategies

SEEING AROUND
CORNERS

Thank you for helping to make dreams come true.
This book is a tribute to all of you who made our success possible!

Stan

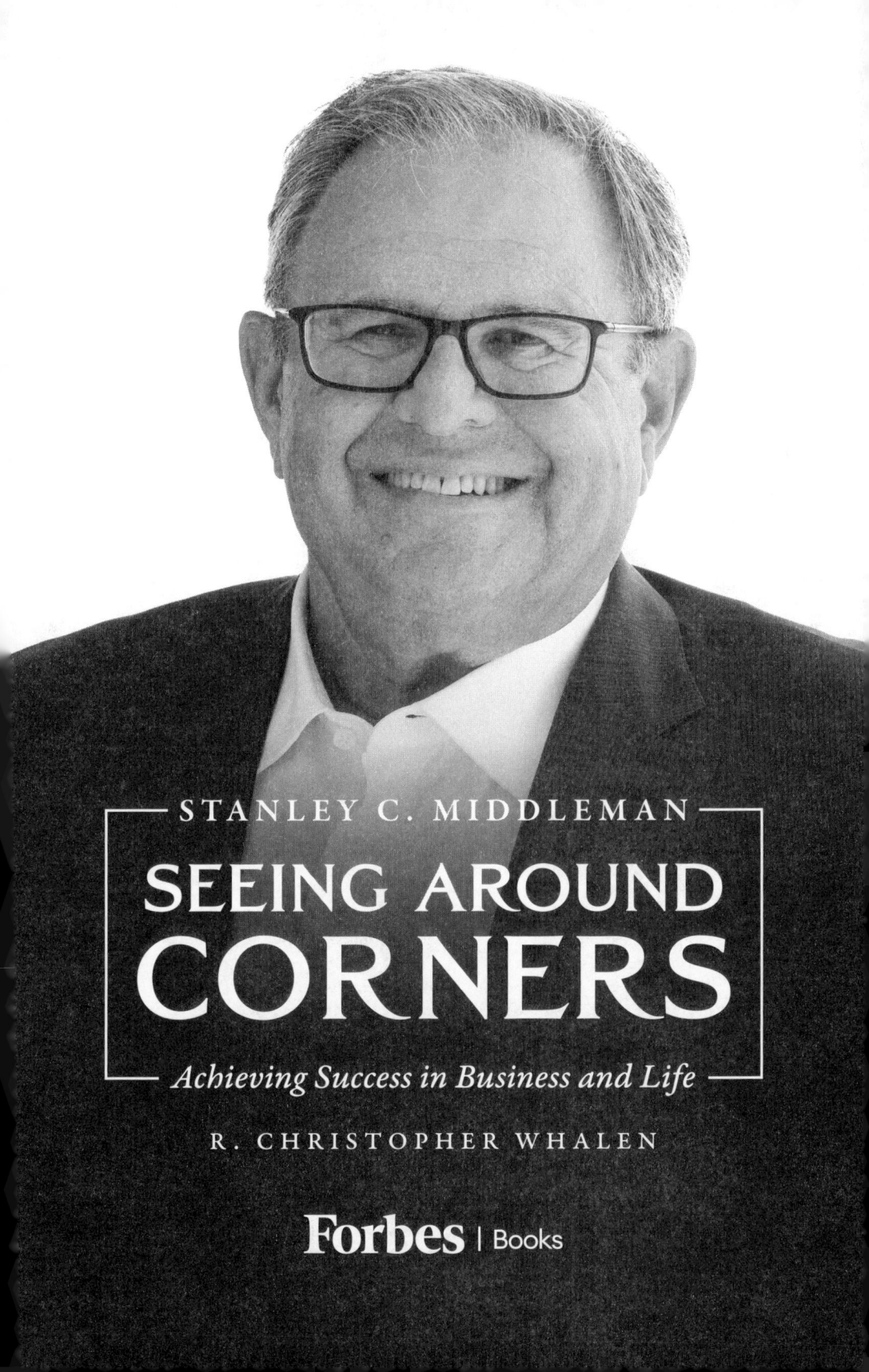

STANLEY C. MIDDLEMAN

SEEING AROUND CORNERS

Achieving Success in Business and Life

R. CHRISTOPHER WHALEN

Forbes | Books

Published by Forbes Books, Charleston, South Carolina.
An imprint of Advantage Media Group.

Forbes Books is a registered trademark, and the Forbes Books colophon is a trademark of Forbes Media, LLC.

Printed in the United States of America.

10 9 8 7 6 5 4 3 2 1

ISBN: 979-8-88750-408-7 (Hardcover)
ISBN: 979-8-88750-409-4 (eBook)

Library of Congress Control Number: 2024904894

Cover design by Analisa Smith.
Layout design by Matthew Morse.

This custom publication is intended to provide accurate information and the opinions of the author in regard to the subject matter covered. It is sold with the understanding that the publisher, Forbes Books, is not engaged in rendering legal, financial, or professional services of any kind. If legal advice or other expert assistance is required, the reader is advised to seek the services of a competent professional.

Since 1917, Forbes has remained steadfast in its mission to serve as the defining voice of entrepreneurial capitalism. Forbes Books, launched in 2016 through a partnership with Advantage Media, furthers that aim by helping business and thought leaders bring their stories, passion, and knowledge to the forefront in custom books. Opinions expressed by Forbes Books authors are their own. To be considered for publication, please visit **books.Forbes.com**.

*This book is dedicated to those rare few people
who have the strength of will to take an idea
and make it into the reality of achievement,
one step at a time.*

CONTENTS

FOREWORD

BY STANLEY C. MIDDLEMAN

I want to thank my good friend Dr. Bruce Levine whose brilliant intellect and burning curiosity inspired me to name this book *Seeing Around Corners*. During one of our conversations, he shared with me the astute observation that some leaders have been able to grow their businesses by having an innate ability to see what others couldn't perceive, that is, by seeing around corners. I was very flattered that Bruce had put me in this category.

He added that whether by intuition, intellect, or experience, these successful leaders were able to grow their businesses over time, while others experienced less achievement. That conversation motivated me and ultimately led to this book becoming a reality. Bruce's memory will long remind me that the insights of others can lead us down the paths that we may not otherwise have taken.

In addition, I want to thank Chris Whalen for his tireless collaboration on this book. After reading his 2017 book, *Ford Men*, I became convinced Chris was the right person to translate my journey. This book is meant to be a review of not only my experiences but also the evolution of the mortgage industry over the past thirty years. I hope this book can contribute to a better understanding of the mortgage market.

I also hope that the story of a kid from Philadelphia who started off with nothing but a desire to succeed will live on, at the very least within future generations of my family. Hopefully, my story will also inspire newly minted entrepreneurs who simply need some encouragement to begin their own journey toward achievement and success. To this end, I also want my family and colleagues at Freedom Mortgage to come to understand my trials and tribulations in building our business and how much I relied upon their love, trust, and support through some difficult times.

I particularly want to thank my beloved wife, Roslyn, and the rest of my family for their unwavering support through these many years of struggle. Although the work and stress were at times difficult, I always had the time and space to dedicate to my trade.

Over thirty years, many generations of business associates, both in and out of my firm, were there to provide stability, support, and a nearly limitless level of inspiration. It was through adversity, competition, and study that we were able to accomplish so much together professionally and personally. Moreover, they helped me strive to self-improve on an almost daily basis.

Seeing Around Corners was born out of a desire to share not only the experiences of my professional life but also the lessons and theories that were formed by those experiences. This book is a distillation from years of learning, trial and error, and revisions in strategy. It is my hope you gain some shortcuts to success after reading this book. Thank you, dear reader, for being intrigued enough to take a glimpse into my life and times.

— STAN

PREFACE

This is the story of Stanley C. Middleman, the eldest child of a working-class family from Northeast Philadelphia circa 1954. It is the genuine tale of an American entrepreneur who failed several times in his early endeavors yet persevered. Through focus, discipline, and sheer personal will to be successful, Stan created enduring achievements. He faced personal and professional challenges along the way and endured a number of hardships. Yet, by always attempting to "see around corners," he created and grew a business that since 1990 has employed and nurtured many thousands of people who work in and around the housing market.

This book tells Stan's story based upon his recollections as well as those of his family and friends. This is also necessarily the story of Freedom Mortgage and its people, today one of the largest government lenders and mortgage servicers in the United States. Along the way, we discuss some of Stan's principles for managing his business and his personal journey as a business owner, a husband and father to two children, and a mentor to many over the past four decades.

As part of the narrative of Stan and his extended family, we also look at the mortgage industry from the perspective of the independent mortgage banker, the sales-oriented firms that actually originate the vast majority of the residential mortgage loans in the United States each year. Stan is a witness to the history of nonbank mortgage finance from the mid-1980s onward. We look through his eyes at the period of change and innovation in the consumer lending business that has occurred since then through to the third decade of the twenty-first century.

This extraordinary American success story starts with a kid trying to sell souvenirs on Independence Mall during the Bicentennial celebration in 1976 and ends with him becoming the founder of Freedom Mortgage, which is today one of the largest family-owned and operated business in the United States. Over the years, members of the Middleman family have worked in the business, including Stan's dad, Lenny Middleman, his wife, Roslyn Middleman, his brother Allen, his aunt Barbara "Bobbie" Pepper, and his cousins Scott and Tina Klein.

In 2001, Stan's nephew Randy Gersten joined the firm. Over the next two decades, Stan's two sons, Michael and Gregory, joined Freedom Mortgage and took on significant operational responsibility for an increasingly complex business. Even as we conclude this account of the life and times of Stan Middleman, we know that the story of focus and a purposeful life continues for Stan and his family into the twenty-first century and beyond.

—CHRIS

STAN'S PRINCIPLES

Throughout this book, we share Stan's strategies based upon his experiences and those of other leaders in the world of mortgage finance. These insights may help you achieve real outcomes throughout your own professional journey. These measurable outcomes are tangible *achievements* that we aim to control through our deliberate actions. In the ten chapters of this book, we combine a narrative of Stan's life experiences with his philosophy on business and life. Each of these key principles reflects ways to help you "see around corners" and apply Stan's experience to your own.

EVERY IDEA STARTS WITH YOU
THEN THINGS CHANGE
THE POWER OF SHARED VISION
IT'S ABOUT EVERYBODY ELSE
LEARN FROM EVERY MISTAKE
TEST AND RETEST YOUR IDEA
LIVING IN TOMORROW

CHAPTER 1

THE GRADUATE

This is the story of how one man with an intense drive to succeed and more than a little good fortune created a new business, by taking risks and seizing opportunities. The business known as Freedom Mortgage was and is built upon the simple idea of helping Americans to buy a home and build wealth, and to use that accumulated capital to improve their lives.

The story of Stan Middleman's long journey to financial success is also about individual discipline, trial and error, and how this deliberate approach leads to enduring accomplishment. In the following chapters, we talk about how focus, careful planning, and hard work—what we call "seeing around corners"—can help anyone build a business, manage the merry-go-round of risk, and create employment and economic security for themselves and others. Stan's life is an important example of achieving the American dream.

Stan was born in 1954 and grew up in a middle-class neighborhood in the city of Philadelphia known as the Great Northeast, a sprawling residential community located a few miles east and north of Center City and the Schuylkill River. He was the eldest son among three siblings; the children of Leonard and Rona included Stan, Allen, and Beth. Much of Stan's sense of responsibility was the result of his mother holding him accountable for the whereabouts and actions of his siblings. Stan was five years older than Allen and ten years older than Beth. His mother's expectations for Stan shaped his sense of responsibility.

Best known for being the birthplace of the United States, one of the largest and most important cities in the country, Philadelphia is also known as an enormous metropolis and an industrial city that helped America win two world wars and build the prosperity that followed. Today, Philly is a commercial center and the hometown for many businesses, large and small.

For Americans like those living in Stan's community, the 1950s were a tough time notwithstanding the growth in the city and the economy. In the 1950s and 1960s, the US economy grew at an average rate of 4.3 percent a year, according to the Bureau of Economic Analysis.[1] Much of the growth in jobs and opportunities during these years came from government spending. In the 1950s and 1960s, money was tight, good jobs were scarce, and mortgage loans were even more difficult to obtain. The dynamic growth that would occur in the 1970s was still many years away.

Stan's neighborhood of Northeast Philly was really the last open area of land developed within the city of Philadelphia, and therefore, the homes are among the most modern construction. The area around the village of Frankford, Pennsylvania, saw a building boom starting in the 1930s, when elevated trains were constructed radiating outward from Center City. A twenty-minute train ride linked the village of Frankford with downtown Philly, driving a commercial and residential home building boom that was only interrupted briefly by World War II.

The area of Philadelphia where Stan's family and friends lived was farmland before the construction of his neighborhood began. Stan's primary school, for example, was brand new when

---

1   BEA.gov, "Gross Domestic Product," accessed September 2023, https://www.bea.gov/data/gdp/gross-domestic-product.

he attended, a remarkable fact given that Philly is one of the oldest cities in the country. He would later go to George Washington High School in Northeast Philadelphia, in Somerton, near a section called Busselton. All of these different sections of Northeast Philly were once rural villages that developed around the key commercial center of Frankford, and all of these communities were later subsumed into the city of Philadelphia.

People in Stan's community had enough to be comfortable but were not affluent by any means. Coming out of the years of World War II and the war in Korea, Americans were heavily taxed and had relatively modest expectations. "We had food on the table, but no money for anything extra," Stan recalls. "People didn't take vacations to Europe or Mexico; they went down to the New Jersey shore or to the Poconos for getaways."

In 1962, the highest marginal individual income tax rate in the United States was 91 percent, and the highest marginal corporate tax rate was 52 percent.[2] That year, a Democratic supply-sider, President John F. Kennedy, announced his plan to introduce permanent, across-the-board tax cuts for both individuals and corporations. That change encouraged the nation and slowly began an economic recovery driven by housing and higher levels of consumption, a recovery that Stan Middleman would first observe and then use to his advantage.

President John F. Kennedy argued that both "logic and equity" demanded tax relief for Americans and that the dollars released from taxation would create new jobs, new salaries, and spur economic growth and an expanding American economy, thereby creating more

---

2   Nick Kasprak, "Some Historical Tax Stats," September 29, 2011, https://taxfoundation. org/some-historical-tax-stats/.

tax revenues.[3] This was a radical change after decades following the Great Depression and two world wars, whereby government in partnership with big corporations and banks ran the show. The Kennedy tax cuts and regulatory changes unleashed the private economy and set the stage for the higher growth—and inflation—over the next several decades. Higher inflation meant higher home prices and greater fluctuations in terms of jobs and interest rates. All of these factors would influence the evolution of Stan's views on how to develop and manage his business career.

Stan's neighborhood off Bloomfield Avenue was composed of mostly single-family homes with some twin properties and small apartments. By the 1960s and early 1970s, areas like Northeast Philly prospered, but still things were hardly booming. Everybody in Stan's neighborhood worked, and each family owned a car, but the economy still reflected the war years and a high degree of government control of the economy. Banks still controlled most of consumer finance and home mortgages albeit with competition from the nonbanks known as Savings & Loans (S&Ls). Stan is a witness to the birth of nonbank finance in those early years of the 1990s, a period that saw some of the highest levels of job creation and economic growth in the United States over the past century.

The local community saw periods of economic growth in the 1960s, followed by inflation and the tough recession years of the 1970s and early 1980s. During the late '60s, conventional theory led to the belief that an "expansive" fiscal and monetary policy could avert any crisis. Reality sank in with severe recession and inflation in the 1970s, when oil price shocks and stagflation discredited the con-

---

3   Mark J. Perry, "Let's Not Forget the Decade the Liberals Love to Hate: The 1960s and President Kennedy's Successful, Supply-Side Tax Cuts," AEI.org, August 17, 2013, https://www.aei.org/carpe-diem/lets-not-forget-the-decade-the-liberals-love-to-hate-the-1960s-and-president-kennedys-successful-supply-side-tax-cuts/.

ventional wisdom about government spending. Indeed, soon the US economy would experience a real estate boom fueled by credit from S&L companies, the first awakening of the nonbank financial sector after half a century of depression, economic crisis, and war.

By the time Stan reached college in the early 1970s, his parents decided to move to Florida with his younger siblings. Stan's dad, Lenny Middleman, had a job in Philly, but he wanted to be his own boss and go into business for himself. The family home had gone up in value by more than double in the years that the Middleman family lived in Northeast Philly, an interesting commentary on the level of home price inflation in those days. President Richard Nixon had imposed wage and price controls in 1971 in an effort to fight inflation, but he eventually took the United States off the gold standard. Inflation won.

Yet, the wealth created via homeownership gave Stan's parents the ability to make the fateful choice to start anew and relocate to another city. His parents took the capital that had grown in the home over several decades and bought an existing business in Miami where they settled. But Stan wanted to stay in Philadelphia for a number of reasons, most of all because he had met his future wife, Roslyn.

"I made the decision to stay and try to make a life for us," Stan reflects on those early years. "As a very young man, I understood what it meant to be on my own and immediately started to look for ways to earn a living while finishing my education."

In 1976, Stan was a senior at Temple University and while attending college, he worked for a large regional lender called Girard Bank, which was headquartered in Center City. He worked from midnight till seven in the morning. A dedicated employee, Stan worked nights at the bank while taking classes full time and also working as a substitute teacher in the Philly public schools. The bank job was in an area called "settlements and adjustments." He recalled those early days of working round the clock to make ends meet and how technology was already starting to make big changes in the world of business:

> My job was making sure that all the day's deposits from smaller banks across the city were reconciled with our computerized recording system. Computers were not yet omnipresent in those days, and smaller banks did not have computers. In fact, there was only one computer in the whole office at Girard. My desk sat outside of the giant computer room, which contained a massive whirring machine. The IBM mainframe computer was enormous. It was raised up off the floor and air conditioned by an individualized cooling system to keep it from overheating.

Computers were still a new phenomenon in the late 1970s. Smaller banks would send larger regional institutions such as Girard Bank tapes of their activity as well as boxes of physical paper checks. Stan and his colleagues would feed that information into the computer to reconcile the transactions. This modern marvel was the size of a truck and sucked in and spit out checks all night, but even in those days, the significance of automation in terms of business efficiency was growing by the day.

Stan was in charge of feeding checks into the computer through the night. He organized trays of checks that had already been added, reconciled, and circulated through the system and then sometimes flew out onto the floor for Stan and his colleagues to sweep up. He gathered the misplaced punch cards in batches and added them up to ensure that they were all counted and matched the computer's data. This work was done at night because all the activity from the smaller local banks had to be collected and then sent to this regional center for processing. Larger banks such as Girard, in turn, would reconcile these correspondent transactions with the Federal Reserve Bank of Philadelphia.

Working in the back office of a bank was an interesting job for a college senior, but like most college students, Stan was still just scraping by even after working two jobs. During his second year of college, Stan's parents moved to Florida. By deciding to stay behind, Stan was completely on his own financially. Stan lived in a shared apartment with some other students and took the elevated train to work. From his night job, Stan scrambled to classes on Mondays, Wednesdays, and Fridays. Tuesdays and Thursdays were when he worked as a substitute teacher.

"My salary was so low that I collected food stamps," Stan reflected. "My two jobs combined didn't leave me with enough money to feed myself."

Accounting was Stan's selected major in college. This was not because he wanted to be an accountant. Instead, Stan early on wanted to acquire the practical skills to understand business and finance in order to become an entrepreneur. This was all unbeknownst to Stan's girlfriend, Roslyn or Ros, who majored in education and who was the main reason he stayed behind in Philadelphia when his parents and siblings moved south to Miami. Ros and Stan met at Pennsylvania State University, and both decided to transfer to Temple in their junior year.

Ros Middleman spoke about that time of challenges: "When Stan's parents said that they were moving to Florida, that kind of set Stan on a path. It was very difficult because he didn't have any money, but he did whatever he could to just make some money and get through. It was really hard, but I think it made him into who he is today."

Stan reminisces: "At that stage in my life, I didn't know what I was going to do after graduation. There were a great many challenges facing us and the clock was ticking. Loudly."

One day, as Stan sat at his desk at the bank overlooking City Hall, his mind began to turn to the fact that the whole city was abuzz in preparation for the 1976 Bicentennial festivities. The city became a destination and the focus of the United States Bicentennial celebratory events. The celebration and events would hit full swing that summer. Frank Rizzo was mayor at the time of the Bicentennial, a law-and-order former police commissioner in the Richard Nixon mold. In those years, Mayor Rizzo was concerned about the potential for trouble during the Bicentennial festivities, but most Philadelphians saw the Bicentennial as a reason for civic pride and celebration, and also as a way to promote the community as a tourist destination. Stan Middleman saw a potential business opportunity. He began to wonder how he could earn money off this momentous occasion. This was the first time in Stan's business career that he recognized the importance of identifying opportunities, of "seeing around corners," to be able to take advantage of a once-in-a-lifetime opportunity before it happened. He set about figuring out how to take advantage of the opportunity of the Bicentennial. Philly was already a major US tourist destination because of the Liberty Bell and other historical sites, but the Bicentennial in and around Philadelphia would exceed that level of visitors many times over.

As Stan envisioned the wandering packs of tourists, the image of a man who had approached him selling hot dogs out of a Sterno-heated metal box at a Phillies baseball game one summer came back into his mind. The man could not seem to carry enough hot dogs in any one trip to meet the demands of all the hungry baseball fans and had to frequently leave the stands to refill his supply of hot dogs.

Imagine, Stan thought, if we could keep the flow of hot dogs moving to meet demand.

From this brief impression, the seed of an idea was born. He could sell hot dogs to tourists on the street, but instead of being stationary on a corner like the traditional hot dog carts, Stan would send folks from a local commissary to approach the crowds as they ambled through the events. He quickly became excited about the idea and began mentally mapping how to make it happen.

All things in business and in life start with one person, Stan has said many times, especially the idea for a new business. Once you take an impression, an idea, and decide to make it real, you create all sorts of possibilities. But Stan learned early on that while many people have ideas, very few people are willing to take that first step needed to make an idea a reality. As you move forward to realize your idea, you must also explore the idea and vet it with other people, Stan believes.

> Throughout my life, I've always relied on the opinions of others to ascertain the feasibility of my ventures and also adjust to change as it occurs. When I get an idea, I bounce it off everybody I know and consider their questions and concerns to evaluate whether it's worth pursuing. I've never been worried about anybody stealing my ideas because I recognized early on that most people like to talk, but they don't like to do. They're about opinion, which works for me since I'm very interested in hearing what they have to say.

Everybody to whom Stan mentioned the hot dog idea seemed to think it had legs. He began contemplating how to build a cart that would serve as home base, the "mother ship" for the hot dog production and a way to fabricate portable boxes to transport the refreshments. The plan was to run the operation like a hub-and-spoke, with distribution at the end of each spoke of the wheel. To Stan, it seemed like a very good idea and one that he had the capacity to pull off, but the idea still required start-up funds to make it happen.

As winter turned to spring, Stan mentioned the plan to his cousin Stewart, whose family owned a fruit stand and grocery store in an area called Olney. Next door, they had opened a small gift shop that was run by Stewart's mom. They sold cards and typical tourist souvenirs. Over some thirty years, Stan's uncle bought the whole block, a very typical success story of a small businessman building wealth in real estate. During that same period, as we noted earlier, the value of that real estate on his street appreciated by double digits.

Stewart thought about the idea for the business and told Stan that he thought it could work. Business is always slower in the colder months because nobody's out walking, Stewart reasoned. "We've got tons of merchandise laying around the store. If you want, you could sell some of our merchandise along with the hot dogs," he told Stan.

The idea of offering other goods besides food was an interesting proposal to Stan. As time passed and no magic influx of cash appeared, he realized that selling souvenirs might be an even better idea than selling hot dogs. He shifted his initial strategy and made a decision to test the idea for real even as he refined the concept.

Through a friend, Stan was introduced to another gift and souvenir store on the corner of 7th and Chestnut Streets near Independence Mall. They sold little *tchotchkes* like tiny Liberty Bells and T-shirts, Philadelphia Phil in a little Revolutionary War outfit, and other items. The stores, in turn, bought their products from "jobbers" who bought from the wholesaler and supplied many stores with these products working out of a truck or van.

Cards and souvenirs required simpler equipment and far less working capital to get started. The jobbers would often give vendors some product for cash and some on consignment. A card table was much cheaper than building the cart Stan envisioned for the hot dogs, so he bought one and hired his first employee, one of the students Stan had met while substitute teaching. But Stan did not realize that by starting this business, he was also entering an established market composed of a community of all manner of street vendors.

In fact, at first, Stan was viewed as an intruder and had a few difficult encounters with other vendors. Sometimes he'd stay up all night to defend a prime spot on a street corner, which was particularly desirable. The tables on the corners tended to do significantly more business, so getting on or near a corner was essential for success.

In addition to running inventory and setting up the tables each morning, protecting prime spots was his most important job. Stan remembers with pride that if you were not protecting your spot on the corner, then somebody else was taking it.

During the Bicentennial, the area around the Liberty Bell was very busy. The hub, the sweet spot, was the corner of 5th and Market Streets, because that's where many tourist buses would drop off or pick up customers from dawn till very late at night.

Some of Stan's competitors ran their businesses on the corner too, and during the busy season would pay somebody to hold the spot all night. Stan had to get his spot before the competing vendors every day, because they also sold souvenirs. Sometimes, the competition would threaten Stan, and the other souvenir vendors would get rough and occasionally pull knives. With Stan's perserverance, he was eventually accepted and was at last able to secure the second or third table on every block.

On the opening day of baseball season in April 1976, Stan set up a table full of souvenirs, which he'd received from his cousin Stewart on consignment. Stan's outlay for the merchandise was only $100, and his cousin helped him with pricing. He told Stan how much each item cost and built a small profit in for himself. Stan then marked up all the prices on the items and used this as a testing ground to see just how profitable his idea was. Stan brought the student employee to a corner at 6th and Chestnut before the ball game and asked her to arrange the pen and pencil sets and Liberty Bell replicas in an attractive way. Then he went in to watch the game. This was a dream scenario for Stan—making money while kicking back and enjoying himself!

To Stan's surprise, when he returned to the table afterward, it looked like nothing had been sold. But when the salesgirl reported collecting way more than a hundred dollars, he was astounded—and he still had more stuff left to sell! Even on a day with mediocre weather and a half-packed Veteran's stadium for Phillies baseball, business was booming. Stan believed that his idea really had potential.

This early success was enough to convince Stan that people really wanted these souvenirs and *tchotchkes* (which up to that point was in doubt) and that he'd better create an action plan for the summer. In the following weeks and months, Stan was able to open thirty stands and employ a couple hundred people to sell souvenirs. Eventually, he began to buy products directly from the jobbers who supplied the market with merchandise, increasing his profit margins. Throughout the summer, he went on to sell T-shirts, pen and pencil sets, collector's plates, and spoons to people who were happy to have these mementos of their time spent in Philadelphia.

By the Fourth of July, Stan had made two times in one day what the bank had offered him to work full time in the fall. In today's money, it probably doesn't sound like much, but it took him what seemed like all day to count the $25,000 in ones and fives that his team earned. From this very modest experience, Stan discovered a taste of what it felt like to achieve commercial success, to have cash in your hand after a hard day's work.

During that summer, the city of Philadelphia changed the rules for street vendors, requiring that tables be disassembled each night. Stan was undeterred. In a July 13, 1976, interview in the *Philadelphia Inquirer*, a twenty-two-year-old Stan Middleman described why he was up in the middle of the night waiting to assemble his tables. "Who's going to take care of your stuff if you don't take care of it?" he asked.

Fulfilling that opportunity gave him encouragement and began to shape Stan's own philosophies about business. But he was about to learn that "seeing around corners," the theme of this book, is as much about anticipating risks as it is about identifying opportunities. In his initial business ventures and those that followed, trying to perceive and identify risks in the world of business became a central focus for Stan and the business he would eventually build.

"My first lesson in business was gained from the Bicentennial venture in the summer of 1976," Stan reminisces. "The key experience or insight was about the importance of seeing around corners. When I talk about this concept of seeing around corners, I'm referring to the ability to predict or gain insights on the future based on our past experiences. Successful entrepreneurs must use whatever lessons we learn, and whatever hard data we possess, to create a point of view from which we may devise ideas and practical strategies, and also react to change."

Every Idea Starts with You

Good strategies take advantage of your environment, Stan believes, which means you need to understand the place where you live and the climate in which you wish to conduct business. For instance, knowing that hordes of tourists, who were ready to open their pocketbooks, would descend upon Philadelphia indicated that it was prime time to figure out how to sell them goods or services. People who have a view of the future and are able to make actionable plans that take advantage of what they see are bound to find some level of career success. But another part of seeing around corners involves understanding the risks in a given opportunity.

One of Stan's oldest friends from the neighborhood growing up in Northeast Philly is Scott, who he's known since the third grade. Scott liked to joke that were they to ever be desperate for money, he would stand on the corner of 18th and Market Street, outside of his office in Philadelphia, and try to sell an apple. If someone pitied him enough to buy it, Scott would think he was really lucky that he happened to pick a time and place where someone needed an apple.

"But Stan," Scott observed, "would take the sale of the apple and think he was onto something. He would buy a bushel of apples and sell them. And then Stan would want to buy a grove, and then he'd envision an apple processing plant, apple juice, and apple sauce, and marketing for his brand of apple products. And that's the difference between Stan and me and a million other people like me."

The observation of one of Stan's childhood friends says a lot about him and the way that Stan thinks about the business world—and about life. First and foremost, Stan has an active imagination and is not afraid to follow through on the ideas he develops. But a key insight that Stan gained over more than forty years in business is that most people are not that interested in taking action. This insight evolved into Stan's first principle about business and life, namely that 'Every Idea Starts with You.' The tendency of people not to act on their ideas is why Stan believes that having the courage and focus to explore and define a new idea is so crucial.

"The successful entrepreneur must be ready to act on their visions, to take risk and perhaps fail, but learn from the experience, reassess the situation, and then move forward," argues Stan. "The successful business owner must also listen to advice and criticism and process that information to understand how things are changing in the market every single day."

Over four decades of experience as an entrepreneur and employer led Stan to believe that success is self-selected. Most people who are successful make a conscious choice to attain certain achievements. Throughout his personal experience and in meeting with hundreds of people every year, Stan began to see three types of wildly successful people in the highly competitive world of real estate finance.

The first group Stan calls the desperate ones. They are so determined to succeed that they will do whatever it takes to assure that they will get what they want. They're internally motivated strivers. Nothing less than success will satisfy them.

The second group includes people who are successful because they are unbelievably gifted or talented. Whether it's wealth, intellect, musical aptitude, or athletic ability, they have an inherent gift that they've been able to exploit through hard work. But not every gifted person becomes successful; only those who truly want it will live up to their potential.

The third group, Stan continues, includes people who were not born with an extraordinary gift but have gone to great lengths to receive training that allows them to maximize the natural skills and intellect they possess. These are the well-trained, incredibly hard workers.

"If you look around the world, you will see all types of leaders who fit one of those three categories and have achieved their dreams,"

Stan argues. "They all share the capacity to be forward-looking, to accumulate the skills necessary to take advantage of their desperation, talent, or training, coupled with their desire to achieve measurable success in their chosen field."

Stan believes that the ability to see around the corner and imagine ourselves as leaders is the true enabler of success for the owners of businesses. The view of themselves in the future allows them to develop, execute, and build tactics around skills and later to develop strategies that let them exploit those skills, which is the essence of becoming extraordinary.

The Couch Was the Impetus

Always modest and self-deprecating, Stan freely admits to being someone who falls into the desperate category when it comes to seeking economic success. He was not gifted in any particular fashion outside of the desperation to succeed. Stan didn't want to work two jobs like he did in college. He wanted to be watching the game, not working the game. He didn't start out with much, yet he wanted much.

"I didn't start off being philosophical, yet I seem to wax on," Stan reflects. "I'm self-taught. I don't think that I'm super skilled, although I have certain gifts. I would say that my great overriding gift is the ability to exploit my desperation."

Stan recognized a dichotomy early in his life. He had great ambitions but saw himself as a very lazy person. He knew that the most difficult task would be learning to manage himself. "I needed to figure out how to overcome that if I ever wanted to manage others," Stan told the author. "If I truly wanted to be successful, I had to be able to get other people to do things for me, so I wouldn't have to do them myself."

The ability to self-evaluate and also self-motivate was a key part of Stan's success. It allowed him to put together a series of tasks and responsibilities that forced him to commit to daily actions that, over time, became a way of life. By focusing on the next step, he made sure not to be hindered in the goal of being able to enjoy his laziness without succumbing to it. Stan knew that he had to work really hard today so that he could afford to be lazy tomorrow. That was his great moment of self-realization. First comes the work, and then comes the reward. Stan realized that being successful is really his driver, the thing that makes him focus on the next step every day.

Stan's friends, colleagues, and family would disagree with his self-assessment and argue that he is far from lazy. But to this day, Stan would say that laziness is in his nature, a fact that drives him to work harder. Like many Americans, he likes to sit on the couch and watch television. He likes to take it easy and spend time with the family. He likes to have fun.

"But I don't want to spend all my time this way at the expense of everything else that I'd prefer to have—all the luxury and the pleasantries that make being lazy more fun," he concludes. "So, I figured out what I could do today to make tomorrow more enjoyable. I think that is a good way to govern your life."

Stan defines success as an achievement that you need to be able to point to, to identify and measure. Oftentimes, discussions of success and happiness meld together, but Stan is not just talking about happiness. Each individual has different obstacles to hurdle in their quest for contentment. While positive feelings are often a by-product of achievement, happiness is not the same as a successful business career or monetary success. Whatever we do to create success needs to have a quantifiable outcome, Stan believes. He likes to use money as a metric, because everybody understands it. Measuring achievement using wealth is like using inches or feet or yards or miles to measure a journey.

The precursor to creating any plan is taking the time to figure out what you want to achieve in your career. You need to know where the corner is if you want to see around it. In the pages that follow, we will discuss Stan's insights from decades in business about getting better at tasks, learning work habits, and discovering leadership skills that enable you to manage and motivate other people. We will also express methods for developing strategies, visions, and points of view that Stan believes are the bedrock for success. Now that you know a little bit about Stan and what he means about the importance of "seeing around corners," we will share insights on another essential quality for success: developing a point of view.

CHAPTER 2

THERE'S NO ADVERTISEMENT FOR BOSS

TIMELINE

1973	Enrolls at Penn State University
	Teaches school; works at Girard Trust in Philadelphia during the mid-1970s
1976	Graduates in May from Temple University
	Conceives of concession business for the Bicentennial in Philly
	Wind and rain thwart the best-laid plans
	Christmas in Miami with family
1977	Meets Clauss brothers
	Becomes manager of Alarms and Locks Unlimited
	Clauss brothers sell locksmith business
	Becomes manager of the Calico Kitchen

The Bicentennial celebrations in Philadelphia during the summer of 1976 were the biggest tourism opportunity to hit the area. Planners of Philadelphia's Bicentennial celebration were mindful of the memorable 1876 Centennial celebration as well as the notable flop of the 1926

Sesquicentennial. In the twentieth century, they hoped to showcase the growth and future ambitions of this American city while also commemorating the two-hundredth anniversary of the Declaration of Independence.

The scale of the activities in and around Philly in 1976 was vast, particularly considering that the city and dozens of surrounding towns and communities all hosted Bicentennial events. On July 4, 1976, President Gerald Ford and Pennsylvania governor Milton Shapp started the festivities by welcoming a wagon train at Valley Forge Park. President Ford said, "The American adventure is a continuing process. As one milestone is passed, another is sighted. As we achieve one goal—a longer life span, a literate population, a leadership in world affairs—we raise our sights."

Stan was determined to take advantage of this singular event. His business model was built upon a basic premise, but this also meant that there was risk involved. Like any new venture, this first effort at sales was a learning experience but no different from any new business.

And for a good part of the summer, Stan's vision for his first business opportunity was proven correct. Indeed, the business took off seemingly on its own and quickly became a big management challenge for a young man with no previous experience operating a business. He had not yet learned enough about business and life to understand what he did not know, the key motivation to seeing around corners.

The first business lesson Stan learned that summer is that scale begets complexity. A business with one employee and one stand could be tightly controlled. In a relatively short period of time, though, he had many stands selling all different products. The complexity of the business multiplied: each new stand needed new people for each table. Stan quickly learned the hard way that more tables were much more difficult to oversee and manage.

In fact, the management complexity and tasks actually grew faster than the number of stands. He needed way more help to manage the inventory and move it around. He needed more products in order to keep the stands looking full. Then he needed more locations. He needed additional people to supervise those who were marketing and selling the products. What started off as a simple business idea became much more difficult to control as the scale of the enterprise increased.

Somehow, with little in the way of capital and a lot of energy, Stan was able to continually meet those demands. Although the process of scaling up the business was fast and fairly efficient, he was suddenly interrupted by an act of nature. This experience illustrates Stan's second principle, Then Things Change, namely that things in business and life can and do change, sometimes very quickly and without warning. The only thing you can depend upon in life is change.

On July Fourth of 1976, there was an enormous thunderstorm late in the afternoon and into the early evening. All the T-shirts on all of the tables were caught in the downpour and got soaked. "I remember watching T-shirts float down the gutters along the street on Independence Mall like mini lifeboats," he recalls ruefully. "The remaining shirts had to be washed and pressed and many of them shrank several sizes. Needless to say, the sizes indicated on the labels were now incorrect. Inventory caught in a rainstorm in an outside business is not as appealing as inventory that's fresh out of a box. Even the boxes were ruined and soggy. I learned that day how quickly the best laid plans of mice and men can sail away."

Even though Stan and his staff were prepared for rainstorms, they weren't prepared for the force and ferocity of this particular summer rainstorm or its timing. He had all of this money invested in this weekend, and the storm brought Stan's venture to the verge of ruin. Even before he got a chance to harvest the profitability from his inventory, Stan's business was teetering. The basic business model remained sound, but that day he discovered that a hidden risk in the outdoor sales business was the weather. This would be Stan's first lesson in the reality that "seeing around corners" was about identifying opportunities as well as risks.

"Risk management is a critical element in any approach to building a successful operation with continued profitability," says Stan. "Preparing to face the onslaught of changing conditions is vital. When everything I'd built washed away because the weather suddenly changed, I was ill-prepared to deal with the risk of things not going as planned. Because I had been so successful up until that point, I had developed hubris, perhaps the biggest risk to any entrepreneur."

Stan was able to weather the July 4 rainstorm, but then he was hit with a second incident, an obstacle neither he nor many others in Philadelphia could ever have imagined. In the first week of August, more than one hundred people who attended the American Legion Convention in Philadelphia the week earlier were rushed to the hospital complaining of fatigue, chest pain, and fever. Eventually, 29 people died, and more than 150 people were sickened.

Within a week, a national reaction to the tragedy essentially ended the remainder of the tourist season early in Philadelphia that year. "Tracing the Philly Killer" was the headline on the cover of *Time* magazine. Suddenly, people were canceling their Bicentennial trips to Philadelphia, fearing for their very lives, in what should have been the busiest month of the summer.

Eventually, researchers and investigators identified the culprit: stagnant water in an air-conditioning unit in the hotel where the Legionnaires were staying carried a deadly bacterium that resulted in pneumonia. Many of the guests contracted that rare form of pneumonia that ultimately became known as Legionnaires' disease.

Decades later, doctors treating patients with COVID-19 also discovered a number of patients had the *legionella* bacteria that causes Legionnaires' disease.

To no surprise, the outbreak of Legionnaires' disease tempered the celebratory atmosphere in the city. Of course, Stan couldn't have predicted this turn of events, but the change rendered his business strategy unworkable. This strange and tragic occurrence had nothing to do with personal failure, but it taught Stan a lesson about how to deal with an unexpected disruption from factors that were previously unknown. It also forced him to rethink the strategy of the business without losing perspective. After the Legionnaires' disease outbreak, the number of visitors to Philly plummeted, and the souvenir business never returned to its previous levels. Stan learned to contend with the decrease in potential customers along with a host of other issues that occurred in order to continue driving some level of sales throughout the end of the summer.

By the end of September 1976, when the tourist season came to a screeching halt, he was stuck with an excess of inventory. Stan: "I found myself standing on the corner, ringing those little Liberty Bells in hopes of attracting the few tourists who remained. As the days grew shorter and the weather got chillier, I was left out in the cold with my unsold goods."

Stan stopped buying new inventory and, instead, started consolidating stands. He went from thirty stands to ten stands to five stands. By November, Stan was still outside in the cold, selling souvenirs to the trickle of tourists who came to visit the town as fall turned to a brisk Pennsylvania winter. As you might expect, Stan wasn't ready to give up without getting back some of the money he'd spent on inventory, goods that were now covered with plastic to protect them from the elements. Everything he had left over would become a loss.

While the risk of inclement weather was remote, the lack of foresight kept him from enjoying the sense of victory he might have experienced with better planning. So, even though his vision of the Bicentennial business opportunity led to wild success in some respects, by the end of the summer, Stan found himself practically back to square one in terms of career prospects. Winter was approaching, and he was back where he had started several months before looking for a job.

In some respects, the end of Stan's experiment in street-level retail sales was a sad ending to a mostly exhilarating period in his life. At the same time, however, it was a great learning experience for a young entrepreneur. It allowed Stan to experience the whole life span of a business, from start to finish, in several months.

Stan says: "It helped shape my point of view about future endeavors. That period of intense, highly detailed focus of activity in a new business taught me tremendous lessons that I have carried throughout my business life. Things can change a lot in business and without much warning, leaving your carefully drawn plans in shambles."

That summer of 1976, Stan learned about the importance of not only having a point of view but also converting a concept into a reality, turning that reality into a success, and then gaining new insights and tactics for sustaining it through changing circumstances. These are lessons that all business owners will encounter at some point, Stan avers, but he also felt fortunate that his first moment of reckoning came early in his career. The summer of 1976 is a lesson Stan will always remember.

The money Stan made during the summer of the Bicentennial was spent quickly to cover living expenses. He used the proceeds from the inventory to support himself, which wasn't going to be the glorious lifestyle enjoyed all summer when the cash was flowing freely and customers were mobbing the stands. As 1976 ended, Stan was staring at a future that wasn't very bright, in the bleak, gray light of the present.

As Christmas approached, he packed up the remaining souvenirs and stored them in a friend's garage. Stan and Ros took the money that remained, which wasn't much, and drove down to Florida in his 1964 Chevy Bel Air station wagon to spend the holiday with his parents and siblings. They pondered their next steps along the way. Stan was a college graduate with a little bit of money but no job. He had forsaken reliable employment to spend time building a business, a business that seemed promising, but then vanished in the blink of an eye. Ros had a degree in education and was working as a substitute teacher in Philadelphia. Things were not easy for the young couple in the beginning, but Stan wanted to succeed in business—but doing what? At least, the weather in Florida was warmer!

There's No Advertisement for Boss

Sitting in his parents' living room in Miami in December 1976, Stan opened the Sunday *Philadelphia Inquirer* to the employment section. Newspapers were the shared experience of Americans at that time, the simple but direct way that people received and exchanged information. Television had not yet supplanted print media, and the internet was still a decade away. Outside of personal connections, there was no other way to find a job in those days. Stan recounts that as he sat on the floor in his parents' home in Miami, reading the paper, his father walked up behind, looked down, and said:

"You're having trouble finding a job, aren't you?"

Stan nodded. "You know why?" his dad asked.

"No, why? I really don't get it," Stan told him.

"There's no advertisement for boss."

Stan knew that his father was right. His dad had taken a chance by selling the family home in Philly, taking the equity in the house, and moving to Miami to run his own business. His father didn't want to be somebody's employee. He had bigger plans for himself.

The benchmarks we create for ourselves are influenced by our families, the environments we're born into, and most importantly, perhaps, our own personalities and motivations. His brother, sister, and Stan grew up in the same household, but they are very different individuals. Each of them has different gifts, talents, and life outcomes. But Stan's dad knew well enough that his eldest son wanted to be his own boss and encouraged his ambition to own a business just as he had done. Stan talked about that period decades later:

> It has always seemed to me that where you were born in the family cycle has an impact on all those factors that determine your success in life. I was the eldest brother and was often put in charge of my younger siblings. I didn't consciously decide to be the boss. But by virtue of my position in my family dynamics, I found myself teaching my little brother Allen how to do things (making him a better playmate). My sister, Beth, was eleven years younger than me so I spent most of my time watching her and taking care of her needs. I taught Allen how to play various sports. He first became proficient at baseball and I eventually let him join my group of friends in the neighborhood in playing in our sandlot games. When I learned to drive, Allen came with me to Phillies games. I wasn't trying to be a leader, just watching and caring for my brother, but

through our relationship, I began developing skills, like instilling pride and confidence in him and teaching him responsibility that would serve me well later in life. To me, that's what it means to be a big brother. My goals were simple: I wanted to marry Ros, have a family, and for us to be financially secure.

After that conversation with his father in Florida over Christmas, Stan took stock of himself and his aspirations. He accepted his dad's judgment that you are never going to find prospects looking under "Help Wanted." Instead, he started looking under "Business Opportunities." Merely reading the newspaper, Stan found several contacts who would turn out to be extremely important in his next stage of development. Stan called one of them from Florida and set up a meeting for when he returned to Philadelphia.

Unlocking Potential Opportunity

The next several business opportunities that came along were from two older gentlemen named Felix and Tom Clauss, whom Stan met via a classified ad in the newspaper. At the time, these veteran businessmen earned their money by buying businesses, rehabilitating other people's mistakes, making the businesses more profitable, and then selling them. The Clauss family shared a small office in Jenkintown, Pennsylvania, in an upscale building called the Fox Pavilion. They sat Stan down between them and grilled him for a couple of hours, but by the end of the meeting, the Clauss brothers were trying to convince the bright young man to join them. Stan described the experience he had in business, including a few mistakes, and the things he was doing to create some opportunities. Perhaps the Clauss brothers saw a little of themselves in this bright and very hungry young man.

The Clauss family included successful contractors in Philly, doing business as Clauss Brothers Contracting and Felix Clauss and Sons, going back decades before they met Stan Middleman. They built roads, sidewalks, and other civil construction projects around Independence Mall and all over the city of Philadelphia, including major contracts such as the construction of Roosevelt Blvd. Trading under the name of Felix Clauss and Sons, they also were the builders on other construction projects, including single-family developments in Huntington Valley. By the end of the 1970s, however, the city of Philadelphia was in a period of long-term decline, and new construction opportunities were scarce.

The economy in those days was tough. It was difficult for people to find jobs and even more difficult to buy a home. America was coming off the highest levels of inflation since World War II, and many Americans were angered by rising prices. In response, Federal Reserve Board chairman Paul Volcker raised short-term interest rates close to 20 percent after the 1980 election, making economic times especially difficult for many people. As Stan and his generation came of age as young adults, they were caught right in the middle of the inflation of the 1970s and on the cusp of Reaganomics. This difficult time would eventually lead to a better period of lower interest rates and better opportunities and economic growth.

In those days, inflation was much on the mind of American consumers. Wages, home prices, gasoline, and most living costs were all rising visibly each year. Inflation was a fact of life for everyone. In 1974, for example, President Gerald Ford declared inflation "public enemy number one."[4] President Ford's economic advisors devised a Whip Inflation Now or WIN program in the fall of that year that initially generated strong public support.

In the late 1970s, if you had a job, you kept it. The idea of quitting a job to start your own business as Stan's father had done was a daunting concept. There was no real labor mobility in those days and no credit except from banks. Venture capital to support new businesses was decades away. People would get a job and stay at the same company for their entire career. Only dreamers deluded themselves into thinking they could be successful in business.

Thankfully, there were and are many dreamers in the world. Some of those people, such as Stan Middleman, turned dreams into deliberate, purposeful action, even in the era before home computers and efficiencies thanks to technology. The big change that started to manifest with new technology, however, was the way in which it enabled the creation of new, smaller enterprises.

Technology gave small businesses the ability to complete more tasks and thus compete with larger firms. In the case of Stan, it enabled him to pursue more ideas for his business and steadily make operations more efficient. The advent of technology and particularly personal computers became a huge help to entrepreneurs starting businesses in the 1980s. If you were tracking a business with a paper ledger sheet, it limited your ability to grow and manage the business. Smaller community banks or brokers were in the same boat in terms of the lack of technology in the business.

As this began to change, however, smaller businesses leveraging technology could suddenly boost their productivity and their ability

---

4   Mo Rocca, "WIN: How Gerald Ford Tried to Whip Inflation with a Button," CBSNews.com, January 8, 2023, https://www.cbsnews.com/news/win-how-gerald-ford-tried-to-whip-inflation-with-a-button/.

to serve their customers in a way that had been reserved to large corporations, mostly because of cost. The bank Stan worked for during college cleared transactions for dozens of other, smaller banks because they had made the investment in large computers necessary to be part of the national payments system regulated by the Federal Reserve.

Coming out of college at that time, Stan and his contemporaries started seeing the major changes slowly ripple through the entire economy. The job opportunities that existed only a few years earlier were very different from when Stan and Ros graduated from Temple University in 1976. The late 1970s were the end of the relatively slow economic growth that Americans had seen for two decades before and the start of an exciting new era of new technology and higher growth.

The Key to Success

The Clauss family was looking for someone to run a local locksmithing company they had just purchased, Alarms and Locks Unlimited. The store was located on Ridge Avenue in the Roxborough section of Philly. Stan didn't have enough money to buy into the business himself. And the young man didn't have much experience, so he really couldn't be an owner. What Stan had in abundance was a willingness to work hard and devote his enormous energy to try to be successful. Stan's motivation was simple: he didn't want to be poor. But the Clauss brothers told Stan that if he was successful in making this business profitable, he would gain some sweat equity in their next venture. Stan and Ros were to be married in May 1977, so this new and first serious business venture for Stan was enormously important. He didn't know a thing about locks or alarms, but he was about to receive an education.

Alarms and Locks Unlimited was a traditional locksmith shop that was now entering the fledgling industry of burglar alarms. New electronic innovations like motion sensors and other tools were introduced in the 1970s, implementing the technology of ultrasound waves. Then infrared devices made alarms more sensitive and reliable. By the 1980s, these security systems were affordable enough for the home or office and soon would be ubiquitous. This was just one example of how technology was making new products and services available and at progressively lower prices and at an accelerating rate of change.

As Stan and his partners became immersed in the world of alarms, they tried to retain the existing client base that was inherited with the business by providing good service. The previous owner had many large accounts, but he was a sole proprietor in every sense. In fact, the previous owner was so busy doing the actual locksmithing work that he never devoted the time to build the business or attract new accounts. He earned just enough to feed himself and his family but never had the capacity to grow the business or offer more services as technology advanced.

To Stan, the first thing to do when you're trying to build a new business is learn the skills necessary for that business. He began by learning how to make a key. And then he learned how to make locks work on doors, how to fit a lock properly, and the other tricks of the trade in home security. The next phase of learning was about doors with alarms. Through experimentation, hard work, and some testing, Stan grew his knowledge and was able to expand the small business almost immediately.

The previous owner of the locksmith company trained Stan on different aspects of the business, and Stan did the daily work in the early days. Then, Stan hired an experienced locksmith to do the actual work and thereby immediately doubled his capacity to grow the business. Stan also employed the new locksmith as a contractor to install any alarms that were sold. Early on, the locksmith joined Stan on a couple of sales presentations and showed clients how the alarms worked. Pretty soon, the locksmith was closing alarm sales on his own, leaving Stan to focus on growing the business.

Stan then started advertising individual smoke alarm units, which paid much more per transaction than a locksmithing job. At that point, the alarm company started to gather some steam, and the business really began to grow. Stan had walked into a business run by a craftsman, an artisan who focused on how good he did the work. Stan's goal was to make it a business that was sustainable but, more importantly, scalable.

The Clauss brothers gave Stan the latitude to run the business, and he almost immediately invested in advertising to grow the customer base. He continued learning from every task involved with managing and growing the business. Whether it was hiring personnel, who brought the expertise to perform those tasks to support the business, or investing in advertising in local papers, Stan engaged in the pragmatic exercises associated with running the day-to-day operations without getting bogged down by them.

From this experience, Stan learned perhaps the most important lesson in any commercial endeavor: hire good people to help you grow the existing business and thereby leave you with time to focus on the next opportunity. This leads us to Stan's third principle, namely, 'The Power of a Shared Vision.' Whether you are Henry Ford or Stanley Middleman running a small business in Philadelphia, it takes a team with a shared vision, hard work, and some considerable luck to build an enduring business enterprise.

The vision from Stan's employers was simple. His job was to bring the business to a place where there were operating profits so that the business could eventually be sold. Neither the Clauss family nor Stan envisioned operating a locksmith and alarms business for the next fifty years.

Stan's job was to impart the vision for the business to his growing employee team. Stan tried everything imaginable to ready the business for sale, from building up the locksmith activity to new alarm sales to ultimately selling smoke detectors as a retail outlet (which turned out to be very profitable). The late 1970s were a period when new technologies were creating whole new areas of consumer services, and Stan was fortunate to ride that wave with the locksmithing business.

One day in 1977, a customer who used the locksmith's services and bought one of the security alarms approached Stan about buying the company. The customer looked at how much he paid the locksmith throughout the course of the year for the alarm service and determined that he could be successful growing the alarm business. In just a year's time, Stan had driven up the revenue of the business, and the Clauss family was able to sell the business for nine times what they paid originally. The Clauss brothers were impressed with Stan's performance and decided to start a new restaurant venture inside an equally new mall in Philly.

In retrospect, this transaction was quite ironic. The buyer of the business was a mortgage company subsidiary of a bank, who owned a multifamily apartment rental community of hundreds of units. They wanted to "insource" the alarm company's products to their customers. This was Stan's introduction to the concept of vertical integration in a business. For both Stan and the Clauss brothers, this was a home run. This success enabled Stan to move onto the next business venture sponsored by the Clauss brothers.

Through the experience of building and ultimately selling the locksmith and alarm business, Stan learned the value of growing revenue and building profitability. Another key lesson was to pay close attention to the work performed each day in order to build your business. He also learned that it was important not to just be good at the tasks but also to be good at executing the tactics around completing the task. Another lesson Stan gained from his discussions with the previous owner of the locksmith business, perhaps the biggest lesson of all, was the importance of being able to multiply your own capabilities through those of others. That is, building a team to help fulfill the vision and drive growth.

For their next venture, Stan and the Clauss family took the profits from the locksmith business and opened a luncheonette called the Calico Kitchen in a small local mall in Cheltenham, on the border of Philadelphia, at the intersection of Route 309 and Cheltenham Avenue. This time, Stan was an equal partner. They split the business into three ways. Of course, Stan was the one managing the business day-to-day, so he was paid a minimal salary to support his needs while building the restaurant.

"Just when I thought I'd really gotten a handle on this whole business thing, I learned that there were still many more challenges awaiting me in the kitchen," says Stan with some amusement. "But the memory of living hand-to-mouth as a student and needing food stamps just to eat drove my desire to succeed. I told Ros and my friends many times: 'I don't ever want to live like that again, no matter what.'"

From his success in turning around and growing the alarm company, Stan now faced a new challenge of managing one of the most difficult small businesses of all, namely, a restaurant. As he came to grips with the challenges of managing a large group of people and operating a consumer-facing business, Stan learned some very important lessons about business and life when he managed the Calico Kitchen. First and foremost, Stan recalled years later as we discussed his fourth principle: 'It's About Everybody Else,' "It's not about you. It's about being sensitive to everyone else around you. If you want to be able to see around corners, you must be aware of how your customers and partners are doing at all times."

CHAPTER 3

LESSONS FROM THE DISCO DELI

TIMELINE

1978 Becomes manager and partner in the Calico Kitchen

New restaurant thrives through holiday season

1979 Long, cold winter of 1979; energy prices hurt business

Restaurant adds "Disco Deli" to boost business

Calico Kitchen fails and relationship with Clauss brothers ends

1980 New year finds Stan back to square one in career search

With Stan's previous work experience selling souvenirs and working as a locksmith, taking a job managing a restaurant was an entirely new adventure. Also, he was now an equity partner, meaning that his cash compensation each month was based on the profits of the business. Stan had never run a restaurant and didn't know anything about the particulars of the industry. But he was willing to learn and willing to work hard—the two essential ingredients of any successful entrepreneur.

The new business investment by the Clauss family was called the Calico Kitchen, a common name in the Philadelphia area. It was a small restaurant located in Cedarbrook Mall, on the outskirts of Philadelphia and opened in the early 1960s. The original anchor stores were E. J. Korvette, a discount retail store, and Pantry Pride supermarket.

At first, commercial property developers in the Northeast region tended to build strip malls, outdoor venues not a lot different from the small-town Main Street of the horse-and-buggy era. Eventually, however, commercial real estate developers started to build small malls with interior space focused on a Korvette's or some other regional store as the anchor tenant. The Calico Kitchen was located in one of the first such malls in the Philadelphia area.

E. J. Korvette, also known as Korvette's, was founded in 1948 in New York City and was one of the first department store chains to challenge the suggested retail price provisions of antidiscounting statutes in many states. Americans had lived with consumer price and rent controls during the years of World War II. Korvette's had inexpensive garments and other goods and was one of the early "big-box" national retailers, which are stores that strive to achieve economies of scale by focusing on large sales volumes.

The mall that housed Korvette's was located at the end of Broad Street and Cheltenham Avenue, between an older, less affluent neighborhood and a relatively new, more upscale neighborhood to the north and west. Broad Street begins in South Philadelphia by the Girard Estates, bisects Center City, and then goes through the vast expanse of North Philadelphia. Once one of the toughest neighborhoods in the city, today North Philly is an example of diversity and urban rebirth. Broad Street ends a bit more than twelve miles from South Philly at Cheltenham Avenue, which is the border of the city of Philadelphia and Cheltenham Township.

In the 1950s through the 1970s, Stan Middleman's family lived on Bloomfield Avenue near this demarcation point between Northeast Philly and the Greater Northeast, which was significant because of the age of the homes and the varied demographics of the different neighborhoods. Cheltenham Avenue was a busy retail area with restaurants, catering halls for weddings and bat mitzvahs and other retail stores. The mall where Stan began the next phase of his business career had an older neighborhood to one side of Cheltenham Avenue and new construction on the other. This area of Northeast Philly was still considered suburban and outside the city center in the late 1970s and was kind of a new destination venue for many residents.

To the Clauss brothers and Stan, Cedarbrook Mall seemed like a really good location for a restaurant. It attracted a wide range of people visiting Korvette's and the other stores. The mall was close to Germantown and North Philly, on the one hand, and Jenkintown, Elkins Park, and the more upscale neighborhoods to the West and North, such as Fox Chase and Busselton, on the other. But little did Stan know that the location of the mall would eventually become a serious obstacle to growing his own business.

When Stan started as manager of the Calico Kitchen early in 1977, all the necessary skills involved in running a food establishment had to be learned and developed from scratch. His primary job was to be the person on location to make the business successful. Stan talked to vendors and employees and hired new staff, who all reported directly to him. The dealings with all of the vendors who supported the business, who had to be paid upon delivery in many cases, were a big part of Stan's job as manager.

Another dimension of the job, however, was dealing with the broader situation in the neighborhood in terms of crime and public order. There were occasional muggings and even gunfire in the parking lot along Cheltenham Avenue. There were also acts of vandalism in the restaurant. The 1970s were a time of social tensions and urban crime in Philadelphia and many other US cities. This reality added a whole new dimension to the job for a young Stan Middleman in terms of dealing with the dining public.

In addition to keeping the customers happy, there was a tremendous amount of interaction with all of the people who performed services for the restaurant, whether employees or vendors. Stan remembers an occasion when a plumber who had completed some work at the restaurant showed up looking for his money. He held an enormous wrench in his hand. Needless to say, the plumber got paid immediately. Stan recalled during an interview that people had a very different, very direct way of dealing with accounts receivable in those days.

"Inside the mall, in addition to Korvette's, there was a Herman's Sporting Goods and some smaller vendors including some kiosks with a locksmith and a luggage repair guy," Stan recalled in a 2020 interview. "The managers in these stores became friends and mentors to me. What did I know? I was just a kid running a restaurant for the first time! Working eighteen-hour days, seven days a week, was my routine."

Stan's main competitors were the Woolworths at the end of the mall. which served food options that were limited to hot dogs and the like, and the Calico Kitchen, a full-service restaurant with a much better product. Stan worked hard to foster a reputation for running a comfortable place with good value for the money.

"Working to deliver a quality experience to people each and every day in the food service business is a challenge," Stan reminisces. "To operate the restaurant, I had to learn about food costs, bringing in customers, advertising, and hiring and managing many different employees (including some who stole). How to keep the restaurant clean and provide a positive experience for customers was a constant concern. Running the diner taught me that the customer experience, including the food and the way it is served, is really the most important part of the restaurant business."

Stan had to learn about cost control and expense management. He had to learn about seasonality and how to be prepared to handle the peak traffic periods as well as how to adjust for slower periods. Learning all of these little details was a very slow and incremental process because there was so much about the business he didn't yet understand. But perhaps the biggest insight he gained in running the Calico Kitchen was how important each member of the team was to providing a quality product to the customer.

"I remember all of the employees in those days, Charlie the cook and the wait staff and other employees," Stan says. "But I had to be able to perform all of the tasks in the restaurant on any given day from cook to waiter to busboy. Charlie was a sweet guy, a former navy man, but when he drank, the quality of the food suffered. Sometimes I had to help in the kitchen when employees were out sick."

In those days, there weren't many indoor malls in the country, but this new phenomenon was gathering momentum in the Philadelphia area, where the suburbs had come to supplant the inner city. Cedarbrook Mall was a precursor to the larger malls that would emerge around the United States in the ensuing years, but at the time, people were excited to be able to walk through an enclosed shopping center. The restaurant opened in the summer of 1977, but by the time Stan had a full team of employees in place, it was the holiday season, when malls were packed with shoppers.

Stan learned to handle and feed large volumes of people and to estimate the restaurant's needs a week or so out. He needed to keep the right amount of food in stock and avoid spoilage. From the start, Stan managed perishables as a key cost for the business. Starting with no experience in the world of food preparation, Stan had to quickly learn about skills, people, and management.

"There were many challenges, risks, and experiences, and not many people to turn to for answers," says Stan. "It is often said that you become wise when you appreciate the limits of your understanding, the holes in your knowledge, but I was still way down the learning curve."

During this period of his life, Stan also had to learn how to be an adult. He was twenty-three years old with a somewhat successful track record and also a bit of an ego. Because of Stan's age, he wanted to completely disregard whatever failure he experienced and charge forward. Like most people, he wanted to focus more on his successes than on risks. For Stan, it was important that other people thought he was successful. Humility was not a virtue he possessed in those early days, but soon Stan learned that self-effacement is a key aspect to seeing around corners. Humility allows you to learn from your mistakes.

"I talked about our achievements and what we were doing right," Stan remembered. "At the time, I didn't realize that all of the experience I was gaining wasn't coming from my successes, it was coming from my failures. The more I failed and the more things I got wrong, the more I began to get things right. Understanding what I did not know was the beginning of wisdom."

Forgetting Fear

In the weeks leading up to Christmas 1977, the business was doing phenomenally well. The mall was crowded with shoppers who were enjoying the festive ambiance and making their last-minute purchases. Customers from inside the mall could come in and sit at the lunch counter or enter the dining room through a private entrance from the parking lot. Long lines formed going down the corridors, through the mall, and into the parking lot. The restaurant was busy all day long. In order to accommodate the influx of hungry shoppers and also generate more profits, the Calico Kitchen stayed open until midnight, long after most stores in the mall closed at ten o'clock.

All of the many transactions in the restaurant were done in cash. In those days, there were no credit or debit cards widely in use, no cell phones and e-payments. Stan didn't even accept checks at the restaurant. With so much cash money circulating through the business, Stan or one of his employees ventured out to the bank a couple of times a day to make deposits. At closing time, a guard from the mall came to the restaurant and escorted the employees to the bank with the overnight deposit bag.

One night, just a few days before Christmas, Stan was coming to the end of a very busy day. About a quarter of the booths in the restaurant were taken, and there were a couple stragglers sitting at tables. Most of the staff had already gone home. The employees were in the process of emptying the dishwashers and mopping the floors when a gentleman wearing an army jacket came in and asked for the manager.

"As I walked up to meet him, carrying all the cash in my pocket, he pulled a sawed-off shotgun out of the sleeve of his jacket," Stan remembers. "He held it up to my temple and screamed: 'Get on the ground!'"

Reluctantly, Stan followed his command. As he lingered on the ground with the shotgun pressed against his head, Stan found himself surveying the restaurant. He saw the remaining customers in the booths and the terrified waitress, who was hiding behind the empty coat tree. Everybody in the restaurant was paralyzed by the man screaming, "Sit still!"

"In my mind, I started to calculate the situation," Stan remembers. "Being a young man, I wasn't particularly afraid. I thought about what would happen if I pushed the gun away from my head. Could I do it fast enough without it hitting somebody else if it went off while subduing this guy? Then I remembered that we had an insurance policy. Was it smart to pick a fight that I really didn't need to win? Logic and good sense told me to hand the guy the money."

Still, Stan couldn't resist the urge to follow up with a snarky, "Can I get you a sandwich? Can we have your shoes polished? Anything else we can do for you?" Fortunately for Stan, the guy took the money and left. He filed an insurance claim. And most important, nobody was hurt during the brazen armed robbery.

To add to the stress of that experience, Stan was supposed to accompany Ros that evening to her company Christmas party. Instead, he didn't show up for the event at all and only arrived home after two o'clock in the night. There were no cell phones in those days, so he had no way to contact Ros. Needless to say, it was a very interesting evening when an exhausted Stan Middleman finally got home and described his harrowing experience to his young bride.

"At first," Stan said, "she was upset because I had missed the party, but then we cried together as I recounted the night's disturbing events."

Despite the unfortunate event, the robbery at the Calico Kitchen was actually pivotal to Stan's trajectory as a business owner and as a manager of a business and people. Having a criminal pointing a shotgun at his head showed how, in a dangerous situation, all of his thoughts centered around the customers and their safety rather than his own welfare.

Yes, Stan was angry and wanted to stop the guy in his tracks. Had the place been empty, he might have reacted differently. But because other people were at risk, Stan felt a responsibility to protect them. He realized that the outcome of this situation would be far worse if someone else got hurt, which is why Stan decided to placate the intruder. Remarkably, when his life was on the line, Stan wasn't afraid for himself. If anything, he was just plain angry.

From that point forward, most of the scary issues Stan confronted in business failed to rattle him. He realized that if there was a dispute, the worst that could happen was a lawsuit or some regulatory action. There wasn't anybody who would try to kill him. Stan's fears regarding potential threats were lessened when he realized that the consequences of his interactions weren't as great as an ordeal as what he had already faced and survived.

None of this is to say Stan wasn't concerned as a businessman with many of the surprises that arose as time went on. He worried plenty. Stan thought about difficulties and sought solutions. But the day of the robbery at the Calico Kitchen was one of those important moments in his career, an experience that has not faded with the march of time. That was the day Stan realized that fear is a wasted emotion. That experience of a man holding a shotgun to his head taught Stan to spend more time focused on solutions, because solving problems is a far more effective way of dealing with difficult situations than being afraid.

Stan learned, as our brave men and women in uniform always will say, to run toward the danger or the problem. It saves time, money, and aggravation. This experience led Stan to formulate his fourth principle, 'It's about Everybody Else,' a life lesson that has followed him ever since.

"Many people are unable to react in situations because they spend all their time looking inward and focusing on what might happen to them," Stan believes. "But the difference between leaders and everybody else is that leaders must be more sensitive and aware of their surroundings and other people than they are to the personal consequences of their actions. The sign of a young person becoming an adult is when you take responsibility for others."

In determining how to react to a situation, Stan feels that the right question to ask is, "Are you doing the right thing for the team and the business?" The people you work with will grow and prosper if you do the right thing for them and for your business. If you have aligned your interests and created a shared vision, the rest will follow. If you're making decisions in the proper way that advances the business and aligns the interest of all concerned, Stan believes, then everyone will prosper from your efforts. Everyone—the employees, you, and your family.

If you tie your view of what's right for your business to the greatest asset of all, which is human capital, then you will be able to make decisions that are good for everyone. Interestingly, Stan found over the years that this line of reasoning typically enhances your personal outcome. "A great deal of my personal growth has been a result of not spending all of my time focused on myself," he asserts.

Stan strongly believes that when you bring people together, you're building a strength that you individually would never have, which is an incredible advantage for everyone. This also is the essence of the principle 'The Power of Shared Vision,' which is defined as aligning interests.

Identifying Cycles

Following the robbery and heading into the new year, 1978, after being so busy that he could not catch his breath, the holiday rush ended and winter began in earnest. Business ground to a near-halt in Cedarbrook Mall. Stan was shocked and surprised at the falloff in volumes. Everybody had been visiting the mall before Christmas, but the postholiday traffic was a fraction of the previous business. Nobody seemed to be coming to the mall, and the bills began to accumulate. The slowdown was badly timed. Stan had finally learned how to hire people and properly staff the restaurant for the holiday rush. But then, to paraphrase another of Stan's principles, things changed.

In many restaurants, the postholiday slump in business means a drop of 50 percent or more in revenue in January and February. Most consumer-facing businesses experience some degree of seasonality, and the restaurant business is chief among them. It snowed a great deal throughout the winter and into early 1978, and people stopped coming to the mall in the usual numbers. Stan didn't realize that not as many people would come to the mall in those cold winter months. He assumed that because the mall was indoors, and it was cold outside, the mall would always be busy.

Because malls were new, there weren't many people who understood the cyclical nature of mall shopping. Cedarbrook Mall was just a few years old, so some of the businesses had managers who had experienced this before and understood seasonality. When Stan spoke with the other store owners and store managers in the mall, he began to better understand how consumer demand worked.

Just as Stan was learning about the impact of seasonality and weather, there was another challenge in the form of a natural gas shortage. Supply problems drove up the price of natural gas for restaurants. Just as the weather and Legionnaires' disease had scuttled the souvenir business, now higher energy prices were threatening the restaurant with cost increases at a time when business was down.

The restaurant used natural gas eighteen hours a day. In fact, gas was one of the largest expenses at the restaurant, and the price kept going up and up. Because of a combination of the weather and gas prices, people stopped going out to shop and to eat. Since many of the costs were fixed and even rising, the restaurant started falling behind on its bills.

"Without enough income to cover the expenses going out, we still needed to pay personnel and have the kitchen stocked," Stan remembers ruefully. "I could only so do much of the work myself."

Stan had to cut people's hours back and reduce shifts, which led to a loss in personnel. He lost some of the most competent employees because they couldn't afford to live on the reduced hours that he offered. Stan realized how he had come to depend on these people as part of running the business, which underscored the value of employees and how important each member was to the team as a whole.

Stan also became aware of how serious the risks were of losing key people. Most of his employees would choose themselves over Stan in a pinch. Even though they liked Stan and he was nice to them, they ultimately had to do what was best for them in order to feed their families. Any loyalty to Stan also didn't stop some of them from stealing from the business because they weren't making enough money at work. Stan said:

> These were hard lessons for me, because I was raised to be a compassionate and thoughtful person. I wanted to continue being that person. I realized that if I was going to be successful, I had to be more than nice. I had to pay attention to the needs and behaviors of my staff. I had to be aware of what they were thinking and feeling, not just what I was thinking. If I only considered what was in it for me, I couldn't be a true leader. Leaders show others what's in it for them, how integral they are to making the business work. If you're always busy thinking about yourself, you are missing half of your responsibili-

ties. That was probably the greatest lesson I learned as business got tough and customers stopped coming in.

It's crucial to understand the ripple effects of your actions, Stan believes. No person lives in a vacuum. If you keep someone because she's good and you let somebody else go who worked next to her every day, the person you keep may not be thankful. Instead, she may wonder if she's next on the chopping block. Even though what you're doing makes sense to you in terms of the business, it may not make so much sense to other people. The changes that you make to adapt to a different environment may make sense to you, but this insight may elude somebody who just saw a friend or colleague lose their job. They may think they are next. Service in an empty restaurant is usually worse than service in a busy restaurant. It is management's job to make sure employees are busy and happy.

The Disco Deli

Though Stan was working as a manager of a small restaurant in Northeast Philly, he still saw himself as an entrepreneur with inventive and interesting ideas. And Stan certainly wasn't shy about acting upon new ideas. This was Stan's first stab at vertical growth and trying to generate additional income from the existing restaurant business.

Thinking rather boldly, Stan wanted the Calico Kitchen to be more than a luncheonette. He wanted the business to generate more profits on the existing infrastructure. The additional income could all fall to the bottom line, he believed. This change would transform this sleepy mall diner into a "destination," even though people were not even using that term in conversation in the late 1970s.

Stan didn't want to have to use the money the restaurant made one month just to pay the following month's bills. When Stan saw an opportunity for growth, he jumped on it. The restaurant had a very young staff of waitresses, busboys, dishwashers, and short-order cooks—many of the people were recent high school graduates. Just about everybody was young, aside from some of the more seasoned waitresses and the chef. Stan was comfortable working with these kids because of his experience as a substitute teacher.

One of the young people working at the restaurant worked as a DJ part time. He asked Stan if he could throw a party after work for his friends. The DJ offered to pay a hundred bucks to use the back room. Stan thought it sounded like a great opportunity. So, when the restaurant closed for the day, they moved the chairs out of the rear dining room, which was a big-enough space to use as a party room. The young man invited his friends and charged them all to get in. The cover charge covered soda and food and left him some money to keep for being the DJ. He drew in a large crowd, which gave Stan an idea. What if he turned the restaurant into a teen disco on weekends to make some extra money?

Stan bought a glittery disco ball and all the necessary sound equipment for a DJ. He hired the young man and decided that the Calico Kitchen would become the "Disco Deli." Voilà! The restaurant was a diner by day and a teen disco by night in the heart of the Northeast. There was a great demand for such a place for teens to gather on cold nights. People lined up around the mall, literally hundreds and hundreds of people. Teenagers from all over came to the restaurant in the mall in the middle of the winter to attend these parties. On Friday, Saturday, and Sunday nights, the Disco Deli was a social center on Cheltenham Avenue.

Stan thought the idea was working out fantastically. He turned the heat up so that the customers would buy more soda. They bought food as well. Stan used the additional business to pay off expenses he'd amassed during the slow season. Because Stan was so excited about what he was doing, he didn't realize that the other store owners and patrons of the mall were not at all excited by the Disco Deli venture.

One day, the landlord of Cedarbrook Mall came into the restaurant and told Stan that he had to stop the evening events at the restaurant.

"Why?" Stan asked. "The kids love it. It's a great idea."

"Because you're scaring the customers of the other stores. It's taking a toll on their businesses," the landlord replied.

"Come on. There's nothing in my lease that prevents me from doing this," Stan replied.

"Well, that's true. If you want to keep doing it, go ahead."

"I will. We're making money that allows us to pay you. You want us to do that, don't you?"

"We do, but I'm telling you now that this is a warning that we would like you to stop."

The landlord told Stan that the lines of kids in the mall were scaring the customers, and even the employees of the other stores were concerned. The 1970s were racially charged times, and the kids waiting to go to the Disco Deli at night were mostly nonwhite, poor kids from the surrounding neighborhood.

Stan thanked the landlord for the suggestion and continued running the late-night parties. Up to this point, the landlord had been extremely supportive of Stan. When he was behind on rent, the landlord worked out a payment plan. Now, Stan had enough cash coming in that he was satisfying the payment plan. Stan thought that was all that mattered. But the landlord was taking heat from his other tenants, and Stan's business had become problematic for the other stores in the mall. The clock was ticking, but Stan did not yet realize the new risks that his evening program had created for the business.

Stan continued enjoying the profits, until one day he was greeted with an eviction notice. The risks he had taken in order to create short-term revenue were not worth the pain of being evicted, but by then it was too late to change course. Just a year had passed since he started running the disco, but unfortunately, the solution to one problem had caused another problem. Stan hadn't been sensitive to how his actions impacted the landlord, which ultimately created a huge problem for him and his partners. Stan had to get evicted, lose the business, and ultimately be sued and settle that lawsuit with the landlord to learn these crucial lessons.

With an eviction hanging over the business, Stan suffered through the holidays in 1978. That year's trip to visit his parents in Florida didn't happen. While Stan was in court trying to save the restaurant after the eviction, the sheriff came in and locked up the joint with Stan's plane tickets for Florida sitting inside!

"To add insult to injury, the travel agent who sold me the plane tickets had a full-time job as a property manager for the landlord," says Stan. "He was the same guy who evicted me, and he wouldn't let me inside to retrieve my tickets. All I wanted was to spend the holiday season with my parents, and I couldn't even do that."

The experience of having the Calico Kitchen shut down by the landlord taught Stan that people who seemed like friends could quickly become enemies and that failure could be delivered by the strangest of sources. Everybody is not on your side. Not everybody wants to see you succeed, he now understood. The failure of the Calico Kitchen confronted Stan with a number of lessons, illustrating yet another key principle: 'Learn from Every Mistake.'

"Some people don't really care whether you succeed or fail," Stan recalls of that time. "If you don't recognize this, you will have a very short career. In order to succeed, you must be willing to fail. If you are aware that failure is lurking around every corner, in every closet, and behind every door, then you will be vigilant. And it's OK to be a little paranoid."

The failure of the Calico Kitchen ended his partnership with the Clauss brothers and took Stan back to square one in his professional journey. But his character and refusal to accept defeat enabled him to pick himself up and begin again.

Stan learned that you must be afraid of failure almost to the point of paranoia, if you intend to succeed. But you must also understand that failure, readjustment, and renewed effort are part of a larger road to success. Ultimately, you must be able to make sure you're covering your ground and anticipating any risks before they happen. But when adversity disrupts your plans, you must reassess your situation and start again.

The education he received running the Disco Deli would become important to Stan later as he took his career in new directions. There may not have been an advertisement for boss, but he had a knack for being one. Stan was gaining the skills he needed to be a success in business, as long as he could keep the risks at bay. But he was once again faced with the prospect of starting a new business career.

CHAPTER 4

FEAR AND CONSISTENCY

TIMELINE

1979 Attempts to salvage concept of the Disco Deli failure

Takes sales position at Penn Life in Philly

1980 Several partners leave Penn Life to start East Coast Financial

Stan and Ros buy first home

1982 Unemployment reaches 9 percent

With the failure of the Calico Kitchen, Stan had to again take stock of his life and decide upon the next course in terms of pursuing a career in business. His commercial partnership with the Clauss family ended, but Stan tried to salvage the assets of the restaurant. He initially opened a couple of Disco Delis in the area of Northeast Philly, using the same concept of a place that was safe and attractive for teenagers. For a time, there was even a location of the Disco Deli down at the New Jersey shore in Sea Isle City. All of the profits of the stores went to pay the rent, however, so Stan eventually realized that the restaurant business was not going to work.

Once again, Stan looked in the newspaper under business opportunities. He answered an advertisement that said, in so many words, "I am looking for someone to learn my business." He took a job in sales at the Pennsylvania Life Insurance Co., working with an experienced broker named George O'Hara. Stan began his journey into insurance by learning the world of health insurance and hospitalization coverage but soon learned about all of the other insurance products including life, property casualty, and annuities. O'Hara was a great teacher and quickly taught Stan how to sell financial products. He specifically taught Stan the value of a script to support the sales effort and also to use in teaching new recruits the business. Stan not only came to appreciate how to use the script to close sales, but he soon took responsibility for teaching new employees, as well.

Stan was comfortable with the world of finance and the people at Penn Life, who were intelligent and motivated. Philadelphia had been the biggest financial center in the United States early in the country's history and boasted an enormous community of financial firms and professionals. His time working at Penn Life was really Stan's first introduction to a strong sales culture, a business where people's compensation was determined by their ability to sell financial products.

Because the insurance policies were tailored to the needs of the self-employed, the offering made sense to Stan as someone who had worked for himself. The change from running a retail business to selling financial products was an enormously important and serendipitous change for Stan Middleman and for the growing group of business associates that he attracted to his team. The economy was tough in the early 1980s, so Stan had no difficulty recruiting new people to his team.

"Once I had proven my ability to sell and to learn all of the aspects of selling annuities, I was given the opportunity to teach new recruits," Stan recalled those early days. "One of the people I was able to teach was Lou LaRocca, who learned to be effective in sales and to make a nice living. Everybody was on commission in those days, so not every candidate was successful. It was eat what you kill."

Stan not only learned how to teach people the annuity business, but he also became adept at training different types of people. This experience training and mentoring his colleagues at Penn Life was a new version of his role as the big brother to his two siblings. Just as Stan had looked after his brother and sister and made sure that they did their schoolwork, he now acquired a larger family of people who wanted to be successful and care for themselves and their families. Stan was learning to be a manager of a business. When George O'Hara was assigned to another unit, Stan eventually became responsible not only for training at Penn Life but also for recruiting and managing new sales associates.

Having the responsibility of managing his growing business unit at Penn Life set the stage for the next phase in Stan's career, when he would go out on his own. More than just being comfortable with the work, however, Stan loved the idea of providing a product that actually helped people. Annuities solved a big challenge facing all adults, namely, how to finance consumption after retirement. In return for an initial investment, consumers could receive a constant income stream for the remainder of their lives and benefit from the pooling of risk among thousands of similar individuals. The annuity industry in the United States was actually created in Philadelphia in the mid-1700s and had developed into a large national industry two centuries later.[5] And Stan, as you would expect, excelled in sales.

Beginning in 1979, he talked with his colleagues at Penn Life, attended seminars, and sought every opportunity possible to grow his

---

5   James M. Poterba, "The History of Annuities in the United States," National Bureau of Economic Research, working paper 6001, April 1997, www.nber.org/system/files/working_papers/w6001/w6001.pdf.

knowledge. By 1983, his partner George and another individual whom Stan had trained left Penn Life and went into business together. They operated under the name of East Coast Financial, selling insurance and annuities. Being a quick learner and also a good listener, Stan repeated the same process as he learned previously working at Penn Life. Pretty soon, Stan and his partners had built up a nice business based on selling annuities, and he began to enjoy a degree of economic security.

Best of all, Stan could now spend most of his time teaching others to sell. The tasks he completed and skills he learned in those years provided the fundamental building blocks for his success later. And the changes that were occurring in the economy in those days helped Stan to recruit new associates. The early 1980s were not only about the deleterious effects of inflation on the economy but also about a terrifically high level of unemployment. The inventory that Stan managed in those days was to maintain a steady flow of new sales talent to fuel the business.

Selling insurance was an interesting business in the 1980s. First, it was a nexus of relationship business, that is, about people. You did business with people whom you knew, and you grew your range of acquaintances by delivering a good product to people. Second, new technology was making it easier to generate leads for new customers. You obtained new leads from satisfied customers and contacts you made through them. This focus on delivering value to people appealed to Stan and motivated him to grow the business.

A natural coach and mentor, Stan discovered the power of building a team around teaching members the details of the business and thereby creating a shared vision for the company and their personal success. He also learned a key lesson from George O'Hara in that period, which was having a bigger team of moderate achievers than a smaller team of higher achievers:

> "The question posed to me by George during this period, which I thought was so insightful, was this: 'Do you want to have one person who can give you a thousand units of business or a thousand people who each give you one unit?'
>
> The salesperson who does a thousand units could leave, which would be devastating. So instead he focused on maintaining a large salesforce composed of all different people. His job was to train these associates and to make them successful, so if something did not work, it was his fault. That was a key lesson about managing a financial business that Stan learned from George O'Hara."

The fundamental attitudes about running a business, a people business, stayed with Stan all of his professional life. He hired as many people as he could and used those relationships to sell insurance to everybody whom his team knew. He motivated people to be successful and tried to use that energy and that excitement to grow the business.

This was not a fancy business, and the people involved were from all walks of life, but the rules for running the business that Stan learned were sound. Stan summed it up: "I had tremendous respect for the principles of the business. We were there to help people. We were there to teach people how to help people. We were there to hire people to teach people how to help people."

That style of sales that Stan learned decades ago has largely died in the age of the internet and social media. As is often the case in most sales cultures, a couple of the strongest salespeople usually closed most of the business and also found the largest number of leads to fuel future sales. This well-recognized tendency of a few salespeople to account for a disproportionate share of the sales volumes was a reality that Stan would see repeated many times over the years.

"The year 1980 was a period of struggle for many people," Stan says of the period immediately after he graduated from college at Temple University. "US unemployment nationally was almost nine percent. The unemployment rate hovered between seven and eight percent from the summer of 1980 to the fall of 1981, when it began to rise quickly. People had been optimistic when President Ronald Reagan won the election and in his first year in office. By March 1982, a year into the Reagan presidency, unemployment reached nine percent. By December 1982 the unemployment rate stood at its recession peak of nearly 11 percent. A lot of people were out of work in that year."[6]

The initial optimism that greeted the election of President Reagan had now turned into very palpable pain. And yet even as the economy reached its nadir, the public did not lose all confidence in Reagan: in an October survey cited by Pew Research, a 40 percent plurality said that over the long run, the president's policies would make their economic situation better, while a third said they would make things worse and 15 percent volunteered they would stay the same.[7]

In 1980, Ros and Stan bought their first home in Voorhees, New Jersey. The mortgage to buy the house came from Bank of New Jersey and took literally months to process and approve. Incredibly, the loan carried an interest rate of 16 percent when the Middlemans closed the deal of their home more than four decades ago. At 8 percent, the mortgage interest rates in late 2023 were considered

6   Michael A. Urquhart and Marilyn A. Hewson, "Unemployment Continued to Rise in 1982 as Recession Deepened," *Monthly Labor Review*, February 1983, www.bls.gov/opub/mlr/1983/02/art1full.pdf.

7   Richard C. Auxier, "Reagan's Recession," Pew Research Center, December 14, 2010, https://www.pewresearch.org/2010/12/14/reagans-recession/.

high by both consumers and mortgage lenders but are still just half the levels of the 1980s.

"It was probably the only mortgage that the bank closed that year in my area," Stan observed about the residential housing market in those days. "In 1980, it was a challenge for me and other qualified people to get that mortgage. Credit was very tight." But the fact that it was so difficult to get a loan made an impression on Stan that would later germinate into an idea and a business.

To say that it was tough for Americans to get a home loan in 1980 is an understatement. When Stan applied for his mortgage from the Bank of New Jersey, his application was the only residential mortgage loan that the bank originated for the entire quarter. This whole bank, one of the largest banks in the state of New Jersey at the time, closed just one residential mortgage in that first quarter of 1980, and it was Stan's. The birth of modern nonbank finance in the United States was still a decade away, so the consumers of that era had to go to a bank or S&L for a mortgage. And the S&Ls had to ultimately sell the mortgage to a larger bank.

"It's interesting when you think about that period of time, going back four decades," says Stan thinking about that first experience of buying a home. "Look at the billions of dollars' worth of mortgages that Freedom Mortgage closed in 2019, for example. Every month of that year, we averaged something like four or five billion dollars of new mortgages, literally thousands of loans closed each and every month. Yet, at this bank forty years ago, I was the only mortgage loan the bank made during the entire quarter. That striking comparison speaks to the huge degree to which access to credit has been improved by technology over the years."

For several years in the early 1980s, the housing sector was as flat as the economy. There was fundamentally no borrowing, there was no building, and there was no new construction, which requires bank support. Financing for home loans came from commercial banks or narrowly focused mortgage banks known as Savings & Loans, which often had only state insurance on deposits. The market for independent mortgage banks and secured debt financing was in its infancy, so banks were the predominant suppliers of credit to the US economy, as they had been since World War II.

In the early 1980s, people were afraid of the future. There were very, very few home sales. If anything, the only kind of residential mortgage lending that was done was a second mortgage at a high interest rate, again from a commercial bank. People found it extraordinarily difficult to borrow money or buy a home. But even in that tough period for the US economy, Stan Middleman and his partners thrived. He discussed that period during a 2019 interview:

"In the very early years of my business life in the 1980s, I was selling investments and doing great, moving up the leadership ladder at Penn Life. Eventually I went on to become self-employed and sold annuities and insurance under our firm, East Coast Financial. I found it easy to sell that bundle of financial products. And I was able to build an efficient program around finding the next customer. Little did I realize the vast changes that were underway all around me due to the steady adoption of information technology would change the world of consumer finance and investments forever."

By understanding the needs of the consumer, what they had financially in terms of savings and home equity, and having an offering that worked for his customers, Stan demonstrated that the annuity product was a solid commercial proposition as a business. He was then able to take that experience, hire people to go out and sell this product, and thereby build the company by increasing spending on marketing. But as we discussed earlier, nothing is forever. Just as the annuity business was really starting to hum along in the mid-1980s, changes in the economy and the interest rate environment would force some significant changes in business strategy for Stan and the entire annuity industry. As interest rates fell, the annuity product became less and less attractive. We discuss in chapter 5 that, eventually, Stan and his partners in East Coast Financial split up the business and went their separate ways.

Preparing for Success

When Stan was growing up, his mother, Ronnie, said many times that she didn't care what profession he chose, because there were successful people in every field. She said, "You can be a trash man if you want. As long as you're a successful trash man, I'm OK with it." And she wasn't wrong. Great wealth has been created around waste disposal because it fills a need. Waste Management Inc. is one of the most profitable companies in the country, an entire empire built around collecting what's discarded.

Stan gives his mother a lot of credit for being right, even though he ultimately proceeded in a different direction—but only after trying several possibilities! When you look around, Stan often says, you can find people making money and building successful careers in almost every sector of the economy imaginable. From the outside looking in, it may seem like building a successful business is contingent on the strength of the idea. But Stan's experience is that the idea is only the match that lights the fire. Without fuel in terms of a clear plan to keep the idea going, it will quickly be extinguished. No, the successful business depends upon not just an idea but also consistency and courage. Stan provides the following example:

"A few years ago, I was at a dinner party," Stan reminisces. "A friend began complaining about how he saw a guy on television who was gaining renown for taking people on pizza tours throughout New York City."

He said to Stan, "This guy started a whole business taking people all around the city touring pizzerias. I could have done that."

"Oh yeah. How would you have done that?" Stan asked.

"I know more about pizza than anyone. I should be the one on the morning news show," his friend replied.

Stan had to stop the conversation right there. His friend at the party may have a real affinity for pizza, but that doesn't mean he would have been able to successfully execute this idea. The guy his friend saw on television didn't just have a good idea. He conducted market research. He went to tourism classes and studied his competition. He built relationships with pizzeria owners. He created a price structure for the operation and tested it out. His vision went far beyond knowing that he really liked eating and talking about pizza. There were many levels he had to pass through on his route to building a successful business that allowed him to support himself and pay additional employees. As Oprah Winfrey is famous for saying, "I believe luck is preparation meeting opportunity. If you hadn't been prepared when the opportunity came along, you wouldn't have been lucky."

Fortunate timing certainly plays a factor in success as well, a point well illustrated by the life of Stan Middleman. But it's important to recognize that success doesn't happen because of a good idea or by sheer chance. Success is about following a consistent approach to learning and developing an idea. Stan Middleman symbolizes that reality. He has a formula for turning an opportunity into a profitable endeavor, which he shared during a series of interviews for this book.

"So, you have an idea that makes you excited," Stan begins. "That's a great first step. Creating a profitable endeavor requires releasing that idea into the market and creating revenue from it. Whatever the concept is, whether business to business, or business to consumer, or a service provider, you first need to find out if there is consumer demand to purchase it. Is there a market? Do other people see the value?"

There are various methods for testing out your idea. If somebody else is doing something similar, you can research their model. You can bring in focus groups and survey them about its feasibility. If it's a product, you can create a test model and offer it to a friend and see how he reacts to it. The important thing is to determine whether there's a real appetite for your idea before investing further time and energy. This leads us to Stan's sixth principle: 'Test and Retest Your Idea.'

Test and Retest Your Idea

To Stan's earlier point about "seeing around corners," he really started in business during the 1980s, a time of enormous social and technological change, when the economy was flat and credit was tight. Stan was fortunate enough to be able to use the change he witnessed over the next four decades, and the national desire for greater economic security, to drive enormous success in business. Not everyone is so lucky, but many successful people are often favored by fortune.

To create a successful business from a good idea, Stan believes, you must know what it costs to make your product and run your business so that you can determine the appropriate price point for the market. You must understand how much money it costs to cover your overhead and create a profit. You have to retest your new idea, which has now been converted into a model, to see if there's *really* demand for it. The ongoing changes in consumer preferences and behavior are a very important part of that analysis. After you have an idea and have converted that idea into a model that you know is profitable, you can have an understanding of a price point where that model can find success. This a critical step.

According to the US Chamber of Commerce, 30 percent of new businesses fail during the first two years of operation, 50 percent during the first five years, and 66 percent during the first ten years.[8] One of the main reasons why businesses fail is that they've set their prices too low. Stan elaborates with a simple example:

> Many businesses make the mistake of pricing to match the prices of their competition, not to the cost structure. Think about Starbucks Coffee. In order to drive their growth and product differentiation, they set prices well above the competition and created an entirely new market opportunity.

A business model that does not accurately price to the cost to create your product or service is ill-conceived and doomed to fail, Stan argues. You can't price your product to the competition because your competitors already have a model. They know the expenses and are probably better at maximizing efficiency than is a new entrant. They can produce the same product for even less money. The relationships they've created may allow them to buy raw materials cheaper.

"It's a mistake to produce a product based solely on what your competition is doing," Stan maintains. "You may find that your product can't be produced at a price that has an appeal to the marketplace. In that case, you have to move on and find another idea because

---

8 Chamber of Commerce, "Small Business Statistics," accessed July 2023, https://www.chamberofcommerce.org/small-business-statistics/.

that model failed. Or you can rework your cost structure to see if you can create the product profitably. Many successful businesses ask this basic question about profits each and every day."

Stan's experience working first with annuities and then mortgage loans taught him that when you have conceived of a product that appeals to consumers and is priced for profitability, you then need to create that product at a small scale. In other words, you now have to market that product successfully and prove your idea in a small and controlled fashion in order to test your cost structure. This is essential, because when you're actually running that business and producing the product, you're doing it often enough to demonstrate that you have accurately projected your cost structure.

"Once you've converted your idea into a working model, married that model to a price structure, retested it to see that there's still consumer demand at your price point, then you can begin to scale your model," Stan believes. "Often this growth phase is the next hazard facing a business. On a small scale, the goods and services you produce are selling. You can market products and have them succeed at certain levels, but when you try to scale that up to higher levels, you get to the trap called diminishing marginal returns. The more business you do, the less you make. Your objective is just the opposite, to work efficiently and improve marginal returns so that profits scale upward with volumes."

One of the biggest risks to any new business is the variability of costs as the business grows, a lesson Stan learned in his first business venture. Losses as a business grows usually come from overhead you hadn't anticipated that is necessary to produce the good or service at higher levels. After you have hired an accountant and a lawyer and rented a facility, you should be able to produce more and reduce fixed expenses on a percentage basis to improve your bottom line. However, scaling up a business can have the opposite effect. When you need to hire more accountants, lawyers, or managers, or you outgrow your facility, sometimes your profits can start to plateau or even fall.

"Once you've had an idea, and you've created a model around that idea, and you've proven the price point and the cost structure, you then take it to scale and build a scale model," Stan continues. "If your scale model works, you prove that you can grow your business in a scalable fashion, and now you've created a plan for a profitable business that can be successful on a sustained basis. The next question, however, is whether you have the courage and the personal commitment to take the next step and manage your business in a world of constant change."

Constant Change

The slow decline of interest rates in the 1980s taught Stan the lesson of change as a constant in business. You have the idea for a successful business, but beware, the next trap that you can fall into is the illusion of, "I'm successful, it's going to last forever." Today, the one certainty about every business environment is that change is inevitable and constant. Therefore, you have to be ready to meet the unexpected and adjust your business strategy accordingly and constantly. The principle of constant change is a key facet of how Stan looks at business and life.

Stan's initial experience with constant change came during the Philadelphia Bicentennial in 1976. The sudden downpour during the Bicentennial, followed by a health emergency, likewise came as an unfortunate surprise. Then came the Calico Kitchen, which taught Stan that change, sometimes rapid, adverse transformation, is part of any business and can—and usually does—arrive without notice from a risk that is not fully apparent. The landlord had warned Stan about the disco parties, but he did not fully appreciate the significance of that event for his business. In both cases, Stan processed the event, learned, and moved on.

"Looking back on the Bicentennial, there were internal and external challenges," Stan says. "I started the business with one employee and one stand. In a short period of time, I had many stands that were selling different products that were difficult to operate and support. What started off as a relatively simple business with one table and one salesperson became much more difficult to control and manage. Then the external risks of weather and Legionnaires' disease arrived, dealing a fatal blow to what seemed to be a great business."

Decades later, at Freedom Mortgage, the risks and challenges would not really change; they've just gotten bigger and more complex. Stan and his team go through these same iterations of managing change and risk, much like the world of technology. They develop the product, change and refine it, then test the product in the marketplace, and then assess the level of success. Develop, deploy, and assess, in a continuous process loop not different from creating a new software product or a chip technology. If you study the world of technology companies, the process loop of development, testing, and refinement is a constant part of the business process.

Being prepared to face the daily onslaught of change is vital, Stan believes, especially in light of his experience with managing a large national business through the COVID-19 pandemic. "Your perception of success," he tells colleagues, "can leave you ill-prepared to deal with risk. Risk management is a critical element in any approach to building a successful career or business operation with continued profitability."

Much of the change that Stan saw during his years in business from 1980 onward has not been kind to all people and companies. The change from a parochial, locally based society in the 1950s, '60s, and '70s to a more global and mobile community in the 1980s and thereafter has not been easy. The idea of working in the same job for thirty or forty years has been exchanged for a world of constant, at times bewildering, change. Stan said, "Lots of people were left behind in that process. But the people who embraced change prospered."

For Stan, the story of the last fifty years in the American economy is about the people left behind by change and the people who kept going and adapted to that change. Each of the waypoints in Stan's business life was filled with such people. Those who had the courage to embrace constant change were by far the most successful. As a small business owner and a big employer, he revels in the number of people who have been part of his business family over the past three decades.

Fear

"During our lives we're all challenged and impacted by fear," Stan discussed during a 2019 interview. "Whether we're afraid to fail, we're afraid to succeed or afraid of an event or afraid of a circumstance or afraid of a person or a thing. Fear is a part of life."

Earlier we spoke about the robbery at the Disco Deli, where Stan had the experience of kneeling on the floor with a shotgun pointed at his head. This experience forced a young Stan Middleman to deal with fear. It also made him realize that focusing on the good of others, your customers and employees, is the most important priority for any business owner or manager.

All good things come, Stan believes deeply, to managers who make service to customers and team members their central philosophy. Fear is being paralyzed and unable to react, Stan argues, almost always because you're spending all of your time focused on you. Fear is about looking inward at what is going to happen to you instead of being focused on others. That's an important lesson for leaders of any industry or vocation.

"You have to be more focused on those around you and more *sensitive*, more *aware of your surroundings* than you are of your personal consequences," declares Stan. "Your ability to deal with situations really has to come down to asking yourself if you're doing the right thing for your organization and for your team. The people that you work with will grow and prosper if you do the right thing for them and your business. If you're behaving in the proper way to advance the business, everyone prospers by it. The employees, yourself, your family, all those around you each benefit from your ability to do what's right for the people and the business, and that becomes paramount."

Stan believes that if you make people—all people—the core of your operating plan, you're generally able to make decisions that are good for everyone. And the interesting thing about that line of reasoning, he argues, is typically it enhances your personal outcome as a business owner and manager. Much of Stan's personal growth results from the fact that he didn't spend all his time focused on himself but instead worried about everyone and everything else, sometimes to the point of exhaustion.

"Ros would literally take the iPad out of my hands many nights," Stan remembers with amusement. But if you query any of the successful managers in the world of mortgage finance, that level of focus and personal sacrifice is required to be the manager of a large financial institution.

By growing a business with sensitivity to others and working with clients and your team effectively, you can make many people's lives better and prosper yourself. You can take people whom you meet and see them grow, achieve, and succeed throughout their lifetimes. This is important to any business leader, and especially to Stan because, during a period of stress, you need to be able to depend on your team. Only by building that shared vision from the outset can you prepare yourself for change, sometimes a very difficult change.

"In that moment of crisis that always comes, if your people have been able to depend on you all along, they will believe in you and trust you, and move to drive your common goals across the finish line," Stan asserts. "This is critical. Your people must believe in you as a leader, to trust your judgment, and therefore adopt your views and your goals as their own. No one can achieve very much alone. The core concept is creating mutual self-interest and a culture of achievement, putting one win after another. This way the team is working for itself. You and the business go along for the ride."

To not be an inspiration to those around you, to not believe in them and to not care for them, is a bad decision, a selfish and self-defeating decision, Stan believes.

> Your greatest leaders, your most successful people in business and public life have embraced those around them to help make them be successful and to care about them and their wellbeing and the ultimate outcome of their efforts. A critical piece of every business is the creation and fostering of a core group of people who share a vision.

Stan is of the opinion that the socialization of the shared vision of any organization is crucial to success. How? You always want everybody to be responsible, to own the outcome. You want to be surrounded by smart and capable people who take ownership of the business, an element we'll talk about later in the book as we describe

Stan's great habit of hiring the best people in lending, operations, and capital markets.

You want people to believe not only in you but also in one another as a team. And that really comes down to team building and character, but having veteran bankers and operators in the mix is an enormous advantage. People only follow people whom they believe in and whom they trust. And it goes back to the discussions with Stan about credibility coming from hands-on understanding. You have to be somebody whom others believe in and can trust, because they know that you have the business functions down to the smallest detail. You have to establish your own personal credibility to establish a pattern of trust. You've heard the motto, Stan argues: "Say what you mean and do what you say."

Each and every day when we go to work, there are things that should scare us, Stan declares: changes in the economy, changes in our business, scarcity of personnel, ability to finance and hit payroll on a weekly basis. We fear the competition, their ability to steal our ideas or beat our price. All of these things are scary, but how you deal with these challenges and how much time you spend rationally determining the appropriate outcome and making the appropriate plan are what give you the confidence to defeat your fear. The ability to defeat your fear really comes from confidence in yourself and the preparation that you've done to face the challenges of the moment. The next step in the process, however, is what to do when things go wrong, and your fear is realized.

Failure to Success

One key point that Stan took away from his early years in business is that sometimes things don't go your way and you fail. Stan's early business ventures included great success and also massive, unexpected failure. Fear of failure is sometimes just an accurate depiction of the way things are, the sudden realization of a letdown. There are times when you will fail, and there are times when things won't go your way. Because failing is the next step toward success, however, being afraid to fail is the same as being afraid of anything. This fear can lead to paralysis and actually can lead to failure when you're unable to create a plan and come up with a solution. But when your fear is realized and things don't go your way, it is the way you approach what happens next that really matters.

"The most liberating feeling is having dealt with failure," Stan believes, drawing on his own experience.

> There is no success sweeter than when you rebound from adversity. There is probably no feeling of elation that is more rewarding than coming out of the other end of failure. It's exciting to build a business, to have ideas, to go out and have achievements. But the most rewarding feeling is from having overcome a failure and going on to create a success. As the saying goes, success begets success. True success is cumulative and that's a critical element in your fundamental understanding of how to see around corners. As you succeed, you gain knowledge that helps inform your next steps and manage the risk of change.

"Spend all of your time looking forward, not looking backward," Stan argues, recalling some of his early failures. The greatest celebration of all is to learn the lessons of a failure and use them as you move forward and create new achievements. What Stan calls true success is the accumulation of tactical achievement and tactical failure that leads to the accomplishment of a bigger long-term goal.

"The definition of success sometimes gets blurred because people confuse achievement with success," Stan relates. "And that's not really always the case. The cumulative building of achievements over time and with consistency is what makes for success. Any setback is merely an opportunity for learning and adjustments, which provides the pathway to your ultimate success in business and also in life."

As we move forward with Stan's story, we will encounter some difficult moments, when his business is forced to downsize and lose valuable people because of a slowing economy or rising interest rates. The world of consumer finance outside of the stable and regulated world of banks is a difficult environment, one of going from feast to famine in a matter of months. As Stan migrated from the world of insurance to residential mortgages, understanding the dynamic between employment and interest rates became a central focus for Stan.

Stan Middleman with his younger siblings, Allen and Beth.

Stan and Roslyn's wedding photo.

Stan ringing the Opening Bell in 2013 for the public equity offering of Cherry Hill Mortgage Investment Corporation (CHMI), which trades today on the New York Stock Exchange.

Stan speaking at Mortgage Bankers Association's 100th Annual Conference and Expo in 2013. The MBA's annual conference is the largest gathering of residential real estate finance professionals.

Stan and Roslyn Middleman with former President George W. Bush and former Florida Governor John Ellis "Jeb" Bush at the MBA's 100th Annual Conference and Expo in 2013.

Stan at a Rucksacks to Backpacks distribution event with a few members of the Marine Corps in 2014. Going on its twelfth year (as of 2024), this campaign encourages Freedom Mortgage employees to provide backpacks and school supplies to the children of active-duty military, National Guard members, and Reservists. The school supplies are distributed through several United Service Organizations (USO) centers across the country, just before the start of the new school year.

Stan with Steve Wozniak, co-founder of Apple®, at Freedom Mortgage's 2016 Leadership Conference. This conference is an annual
event that brings together the executive team, high-performing
employees, industry leaders, and celebrity guests to share insights
about the company and the ever-changing mortgage industry. During
this three-day conference, attendees network and learn from notable
speakers about various topics, including politics, leadership, and more.

Stan and Freedom Mortgage received the Liberty United Service Organizations' (USO) esteemed 2018 Chairman's Award in honor of their service to the military community and their support of Liberty USO. The award recognized Freedom Mortgage for making a difference in southern New Jersey and Pennsylvania.

Stan and Roslyn with Nick Foles, former Philadelphia Eagles quarter-
back, as well as Suzy Kolber, former ESPN sports anchor and reporter,
at Freedom Mortgage's 2018 Leadership Conference.

Stan, Roslyn, Lenny, Ronnie, and Michael with Robin Roberts, former anchor for ABC's Good Morning America, and Earvin "Magic" Johnson, Jr., entrepreneur and former point guard for the Los Angeles Lakers of the National Basketball Association (NBA), at Freedom Mortgage's 2019 Leadership Conference.

Stan, Roslyn, Michael, and Greg opening the Stanley Middleman Center for Jewish Life – Rohr Chabad at Temple University (September 13, 2021). To the left of Stan is Temple President Dr. Jason Wingard, as well as Rabbi Baruch and Chanie Kantor, directors of the center. The Center serves as a "home away from home" for Jewish students at Temple.

Stan with his two sons, Michael and Greg, alongside Freedom Mortgage Executives David Sheeler and Mike Patterson, Live Nation Executives Geoff Gordon and Chris Collins, and the lead singer of Train, Pat Monahan, as they officially unveiled the Freedom Mortgage Pavilion in the summer of 2022. Freedom Mortgage is the name-in-title sponsor of the Live Nation Entertainment, indoor/outdoor, 25,000-person capacity amphitheater in Camden, New Jersey.

Stan and Madeline Bell, CEO of the Children's Hospital of Philadelphia (CHOP), in front of the Middleman Family Pavilion at the ribbon-cutting event in 2023. Stan and his family made a personal donation to support the opening of CHOP's second hospital, in King of Prussia, Pennsylvania, in 2022. The Middleman Family Pavilion offers more than 250,000 square feet of space, dedicated to the care of children.

Stan with wife, sons, daughter-in-law, and grandchildren at the Middleman Family Pavilion. Stan is on the Children's Hospital of Philadelphia (CHOP) Foundation Board of Advisors.

Stan with many of Freedom Mortgage's Executive Leadership Team at the Philadelphia Museum of Art in December of 2023.

Top: The Middleman family at the 2023 Phillies Owners' Party, celebrating Stan becoming an official team owner. Stan has been an investor and the vice chairman of the team since 2023.

Left: While supporting his hometown baseball team, Stan received some attention from Phillie Phanatic, the team's mascot.

CHAPTER FIVE

FROM ANNUITIES TO MORTGAGES

TIMELINE

1981 Interest rates soar to high double digits, drive annuities business

1983 Interest rates start to fall

1985 Michael Middleman is born

Stan struck out on his own, focusing on mortgages

Citibank launches no-doc Mortgage Power product

Stan was still a young man when he began his career in finance in the 1980s. He saw a number of financial and political events during a period when America's economic fortune was not considered certain by any means. He and his business associates saw interest rates run wild, and the nation tasted inflation in a serious way for the first time in generations. Interest rates became one of the most significant factors that followed Stan Middleman and other lenders for the next forty years and more.

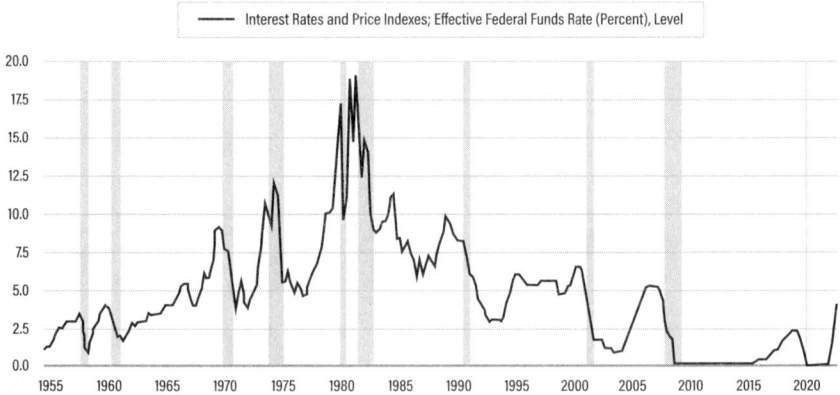

Figure 5.1. Source: Board of Governors of the Federal Reserve System (US), fred.stlouisfed.org.

Americans were shocked by the upward movement in wages and consumer prices during those early years of the 1980s and the strong response by Federal Reserve Board chairman Paul Volcker. "The Great Inflation was the defining macroeconomic period of the second half of the twentieth century," wrote Michael Bryan of the Atlanta Federal Reserve Bank in his essay, "The Great Inflation."[9] "Lasting from 1965 to 1982, it led economists to rethink the policies of the Fed and other central banks." And the major policy trend followed by the Federal Open Market Committee (FOMC) since the 1980s was to use progressively lower interest rates to meet the employment goals set by Congress.

The reality of inflation was very visible in the housing market—for Stan, both as a consumer and as someone making a business originating mortgages. Stan saw that as interest rates fell, mortgages became more affordable and demand increased. Mortgage rates had skyrocketed to as high as 16 percent in 1981. As we discussed in the

9   Michael Bryan, "The Great Inflation," Federal Reserve History, November 22, 2013, https://www.federalreservehistory.org/essays/great-inflation.

last chapter, many people who wanted to buy houses during this period were unable to secure a mortgage. The S&Ls that had historically supported the housing market were decimated by the high interest rates used by Fed chairman Volcker to fight inflation. In those days, commercial banks were reluctant to lend for single-family homes or even commercial properties!

"One of the reasons that I view interest rates as a key indicator of future business trends is my experience during those dark days in the early 1980s," Stan recalled in a discussion about how he thinks about business.

> Over thirty years in the mortgage business, I have come to believe that if you are alert and sensitive, and you pay attention to your surroundings in terms of consumers and other businesses, you can become successful. Our business is mortgage lending, so I try to see the connectivity between things like the economy and interest rates. There are connections between events and where we are in the economic cycle that are clear and fairly predictive, but you must be constantly attentive to the changes around you.

The entire country was dealing with changes in inflation and interest rates that were very different from the decades immediately after World War II, when the government tightly controlled interest rates and most consumer prices. The Federal Reserve even pegged interest rates for much of the period of World War II at the behest of the Treasury, an arrangement that lasted until the 1950s. Three decades later, the whole country was focused on rising inflation on wages and prices, including energy prices, and also interest rates, but this trend also impacted investment returns, a fact that was not lost on Stan Middleman.

"This very tall guy in Washington named Paul Volcker, who had worked for Chase Bank and smoked an enormous cigar, seemed to be in charge," Stan remembers.

> But by 1983, interest rates finally began to fall. I refinanced my house with a 12 percent adjustable-rate mortgage, which left me with a 25 percent lower monthly payment than I had paid previously. This was a huge change for consumers who could actually qualify for a mortgage. I thought it was the greatest thing to ever happen. It freed up a lot of money for me. I was able to create a better life for myself and my family. My cash flow was greater, and it was easier to manage all my expenses because my monthly mortgage payment went down, which was really important to me. But while interest rates did eventually fall from the peaks between 1979–1981, by today's standards interest rates remained relatively high in the 1980s and actually rose higher than 10 percent in 1985.

The following chart shows the federal funds rate during the 1980s.

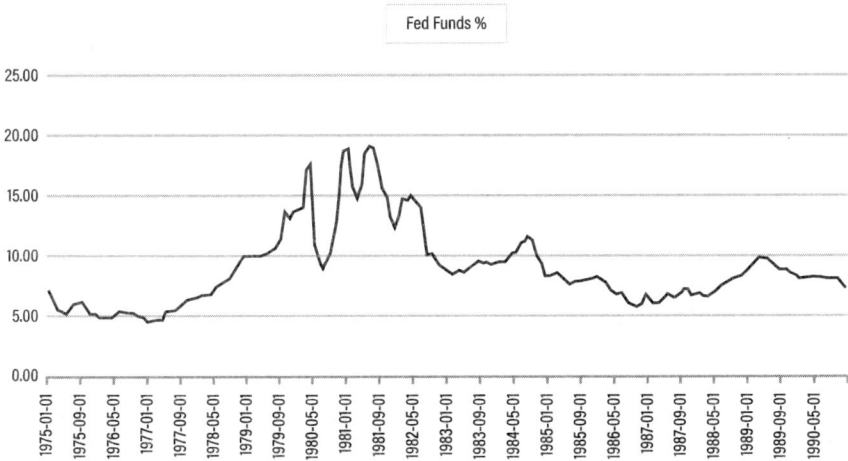

Figure 5.2. Source: FRED.

While lower interest rates were good for Stan's personal finances and for the mortgage market generally, they began to cut into the profitability of selling annuities. Just as higher interest rates had made annuities an easy sell, falling rates had the opposite effect, forcing Stan to reconsider the model for his business.

As interest rates fell, people had more investment options. There wasn't as clear an advantage to buying annuities as there had been a few years back. By 1985, interest rates fell down to a fixed rate of only about 10 or 11 percent, compared to near 20 percent a few years before.

During and after the period of sky-high interest rates, Stan began to ponder the opportunities available in the mortgage market. He knew from his own experience that the mortgage market was closed to most consumers. The home mortgages generated between 1980 and 1985 had higher interest rates and would eventually be refinanced into lower coupon mortgages. By being sensitive to the market climate around him and being aware of the novel demands for financial solutions coming from consumers in the new economic environment, Stan began to shape an idea for a new business.

He deduced that there was a reciprocal relationship between selling annuities, which were now getting diminishing marginal returns, and marketing residential mortgages. Stan loved the idea of using a savings product like an annuity to build household wealth, but he also learned an important lesson to change his sales message with the market. Stan reflects on that period:

> Instead of digging my heels in and sticking with the old business model which had worked so well for me, I recognized that it was time to refocus and take advantage of the new economic climate. I entered the housing finance business as a mortgage broker. My premise was that we could take all the people who had a mortgage today, refinance them into a short-term mortgage, and get them to buy an annuity. Based on the equity on their home, they could borrow more than they owed and build a nice investment return while paying off the house faster.

His firm developed a new offering, and the pitch went something like this: we can reduce the length of your mortgages from thirty years to fifteen years and keep the monthly payments the same. You've already shown that you can afford the payments. The idea was that the client would pay off their house in fifteen years and end up with a greater amount of savings in their annuity, possibly as much as $100,000. The borrower could pay off their house and live debt free with a sizable amount of money put away.

For Stan, combining the annuity product with a shorter mortgage seemed like a great way to boost sales and also help people accumulate wealth. Having come from a modest background, Stan saw the value of helping other working American families build home equity and put money in the bank as a powerful way to improve their lives. His parents had used the equity accumulated in their home in Northeast Philly to move to Miami and buy a business, so Stan understood the power of using leverage in one's home to build wealth. This powerful idea of using leverage to help consumers via homeownership became a core tenet for Stan's new business of combining mortgage lending and annuities.

Stan thought this product offering was a great idea, but he wanted to test it out with other people. He went up and down the block and visited neighbors, most of whom had moved in after Stan had bought his house, when mortgages became easier to get. He talked to seven people, which was certainly not a statistically significant sample, and every one of them thought the idea of refinancing into a short-term mortgage and buying an annuity sounded promising.

So, with this positive initial response, Stan began putting together a plan to make this idea a reality. He did research in order to devise price points and build a model to prove that this concept could work. Once he was ready to go to market, Stan was able to do business with four of the seven people whom he had contacted on his block. For Stan, it was pretty exciting to be able to help these people pay off their houses early and create a plan to build wealth. And he was even more excited about establishing a new business that was relevant to the current economic climate.

As we've discussed, you have to keep validating your ideas as you proceed in building a new business. Stan tried to grow this new model for mortgages with annuities to scale, but he found out that what seemed to be a good idea was a little more complicated when he tried to take it to the next level of validation.

It turned out that it was a lot harder to get people to understand the concept of the annuity and invest in it than it was to convince them to lower their mortgage interest rates and pay off their house sooner. And as Stan began to reach out to a broader population and try to make a real business out of this concept, he discovered that the inclusion of the annuity was killing many potential sales for his firm.

There was also another data point for his analysis: Stan was making more money on the mortgages than he was making on the annuities. The annuities were not only muddying the water and diminishing people's confidence in his product, but they were also hurting sales overall. The annuity sales took more time and generated less profit. People didn't believe Stan about the savings potential of the annuity. Many people simply decided to refinance their mortgages and keep the cash. Indeed, many customers thought simply refinancing the home was too good to be true.

Use Leverage to Build Wealth

Faced with a growing body of data from his sales effort, Stan adapted and changed. In 1985, in a fateful but ultimately necessary turn in his career as a business owner, Stan decided to gradually get out of the annuity business with his partners and start a new business focused on the mortgage product exclusively. By that time, the firm had two offices, one in Cherry Hill and the other in Woodbridge, so Stan took over the latter and created a new firm called United Financial focused on the mortgage business.

Stan's focus was on developing a business to help the homeowner to use the leverage in their house to build wealth. By eventually exiting the annuity business, he didn't have to worry about the investment part of the equation. The homeowner could decide how to use the capital that was released by paying off their mortgage more quickly. This was a huge epiphany for Stan and helped him focus his new business of making mortgage loans. Stan thinks back on that time:

> My pitch evolved. The sales message was simple: By shortening their mortgage at the same rate, they could add years to their ability to live free of mortgage debt if they chose. I took note of falling interest rates and identified an opportunity for people to continue living in the same house and take cash out of their house and invest it, while keeping their monthly payments the same. The theory was that they would end up with more money for their retirement than they would have had otherwise. And my theory was proven correct.

During this time, almost every residential mortgage originated in the United States was a thirty-year mortgage, with extremely high monthly payments and fees. By the mid-1980s, average interest rates on a home loan could be anywhere from 10 to 15 percent, so there was a great demand for lower interest rates and lower ownership costs overall for housing. But with property values rising because of actual and *expected* inflation, people also had increasing equity in their homes. As credit became more available, consumers were suddenly able to leverage that growing value and get rates of return on their home equity that were phenomenal compared to earnings on investments in prior periods. The fact of inflation boosted home prices as well as household wealth, a fact that would carry Stan's new business.

Inflation began ratcheting upward in the mid-1960s and reached more than 14 percent in 1980, however it eventually declined to average only 3.5 percent in the latter half of the 1980s.

As high interest rates fell, the demand for mortgage loans increased. People who already had loans with double-digit annual rates wanted to refinance with lower interest rate loans. Families that wanted to buy homes found that it had become more affordable because their monthly payments would be lower. Because of inflation, more people suddenly discovered that they had buying power as the cost of credit declined, in some cases unlocking significant hidden equity in their homes. They were now able to leverage that larger equity to move into newer, nicer, bigger houses in order to better accommodate their growing families.

Pretty much anybody—including working-class and lower-middle-class people—who were prudent with their money could develop a nest egg in their home equity. The value increases in their homes and their ability to earn high interest rates on their savings were powerful wealth creators. As Stan spoke with potential customers, he wanted to market products that would help them benefit from that powerful synergy between inflation and home prices.

The idea of building household wealth around the equity in the home was a story worth telling. Stan began hiring people to market the concept and develop leads, often using the networking skills he'd developed in selling annuities. His mission was to build the business by utilizing an army of salespeople to tell the story. Since unemployment was high at the time, as mentioned, there were plenty of people available to increase sales. The baby boomers were flooding into the workforce, so there was a slew of young people available to help grow the economy. During this period, Stan met an executive named Larry Jones who had worked for several large companies in New Jersey. Like Stan, Larry really wanted to have his own business. Jones joined Stan at United Financial and became a second manager in the business who could develop a sales script for their associates and train new recruits.

"Larry Jones was one of my earliest colleagues who was focused and also a terrific guy," Stan remembers. "Larry worked for me at United Financial and then at Freedom Mortgage for three decades and was a real stalwart, somebody you could depend upon to get things right. He helped with recruiting and training, but more than anything else, Larry was a seasoned executive who helped me build an enduring business."

The jobs that young people found in the mortgage business were completely different from what their parents had experienced only a couple of decades before. There were literally generations of people in the greater Philadelphia area who had worked for large companies virtually their entire lives. From the 1970s onward, high-paying manufacturing jobs in Philadelphia and South Jersey, jobs that had existed for decades, started to disappear. Factory work and other types of manual labor declined, some moving overseas and some requiring fewer workers because of technological advances.

Working-class folks who had built middle-class lifestyles with good blue-collar jobs were now starting to look for white-collar jobs, which had an enormous impact on society. The rise of technology as the key driver in the world of business and commerce would forever change the definition of the American dream. A big component of this change included homeownership. Stan observes of that period:

> This period during the mid-1980s was the precursor
> to where we are today. Many people, myself included,
> were eager to develop new skills and business experience

in order to persevere in a fast-changing world. Calcula-
tors, computers, and all kinds of work tool aids became
available over the next several years, which revolutionized
the way business worked, both in terms of speed and
complexity. The economy was starting to embrace that
transformational change via technology—a process that
would last decades. As interest rates began to fall and the
value of housing assets rose, increasing personal wealth
for millions, the economy began to pick up steam. We
saw growth in value and wealth via homeownership that
hadn't been created on such a scale for many years. What
the economists call the "wealth effect" truly came into
vogue in those days of the 1980s. That was an exciting
time to be in business, and it was an exciting time to own
a home and to invest and get handsome returns.

Stan's growing company began to tell the story of accessing the
equity in your home. Although the benefits were clear to them, the
products didn't appeal instantly to all homeowners. Even though he
could successfully lower people's interest rates on their mortgages,
the idea of taking additional money out to invest had lost its luster
for some. Many people were conservative when it came to money
and still inclined to keep the equity value in their homes. They were
reluctant to trust the market and to trust investments compared to
simply letting the home equity increase. And in those days, when
home values were rising with inflation, they were probably right.

The Depression Mentality

In his sales effort in and around the Philadelphia area, the older folks Stan encountered were accustomed to keeping money in their mattresses very literally because they had so little trust in the banks.

Much of America boomed economically in the 1920s because of technological progress like mass production of goods and the electrification, but Philly suffered as a production center after the end of World War I when the coal industry slumped, adding to the pressure on employment and the economy.

Coming out of the deflation and weak employment of the post–World War I period, Philly had actually been in a depression long before the 1929 market crash. There was still a lot of scar tissue left in the community from the Great Depression, pain that carried over to children who grew up during that era. Stan called this fear "depression mentality."

The descendants of the Depression-era children, a.k.a. the baby boomers, saw the opportunities in leverage and consumer spending, even though they were raised in a very conservative environment. By the middle of the 1980s, Stan saw more investment properties and more homes being built in Philadelphia. This period of boom times would end, of course, but not until he had established a pretty good understanding of how to make a mortgage.

The impact of both interest rates and the growing economy in the mid-1980s was evident in the growth of Stan's mortgage brokerage business. Customer demand ballooned and with it the business volumes, from one mortgage per quarter to fifteen mortgage applications taken in a day. People believed in the concepts that Stan was selling, and he sold a great deal of home mortgages for a tiny firm with little capital other than sweat equity. Mortgage lending was still a predominantly bank-dominated business, and the independent mortgage brokers like Stan Middleman really had to hustle to win business.

Because his business expanded, moving all the paper around to get credit approvals and collect the necessary information to build credit files became more and more challenging. With the equipment and staff that Stan had, it took anywhere from 120 to 180 days to build the file for a mortgage loan and sometimes even longer. Stan wanted customers to be able to take advantage of this fertile economic environment, but the loan underwriting and approval process moved at a snail's pace. His experience working at Girard Bank as a college student had taught Stan the enormous potential of technology, but the mortgage industry was still manufacturing residential mortgages by hand. Stan remembers that period with amusement:

> In 1985, computers still were not part of the day-to-day world. Word processors were beginning to appear in larger firms. At that time, though, typewriters and carbon paper still reigned supreme. We thought that "Wite-Out" fluid to correct typing errors on a physical piece of paper was a tremendous advancement in technology. Most of the work we did was sent through the mail. We would send a verification to the employer or to the bank or the lienholder and have to wait for a letter back, which meant that processing transactions took an overwhelmingly long time.

As Stan started to need appraisals on these properties, he found there weren't many property appraisers available. There were practically no skilled underwriters. There weren't any really experienced loan processors, because the industry had been inactive for so long.

However, there were plenty of typists available. Stan had to embrace the pool of workers he could find, educate them, and help them build the skill sets that were required.

To meet the need for more people to handle ever more paper in a growing firm, Stan's firm ended up hiring entire classes out of a local business school, which really meant typists, but they were young and bright. The people who enrolled in business school after high school were mainly young women who were developing skills by learning to be typists or administrative assistants. Stan and his managers needed to develop their communications skills and training to be able to address not just individual employees but also large groups. Not only was Stan focused on finding good people, but he also had to retain those people whom he recruited and trained. In order to keep good people, Stan reflected years later, they had to believe in what you were trying to do. He had to give his employees a sense that they were trying to accomplish something extraordinary.

Stan eventually added a second office to United Financial on Route 130 in Pennsauken, New Jersey, helping him to drive growth. This was a significant step for Stan and would lead to the hiring of Maria Gallucci, who would become a key financial officer in United Financial. Maria and Larry Jones were the nucleus of the company in those early days and eventually of Freedom Mortgage.

Soon Stan's firm had rooms that were thousands of square feet, which were filled with row upon row of typists. They filled trash cans with carbon paper. Federal Express, which started in the early 1970s, was brand new and hadn't yet taken hold. There were no fax machines or email. At the end of the day, Stan's employees collected the mail, weighed it, and stamped it. Every night, someone took a trip to the post office.

In those early days of the modern mortgage origination process, Stan built a manufacturing process—what is called today in the industry a loan origination system, or "LOS." The LOS for mortgage loans is focused on creating the credit file with the information about the borrower that will eventually be approved for funding by the correspondent bank. The process was intensely paper oriented and manually constructed. It took a long time for each transaction, because the files created were between three and six inches thick. These bundles of paper were then transported to the bank, usually an S&L, where they were manually reviewed and then approved. At that point, the S&L made the commitment to fund the mortgage, and then the home sale closed.

The S&L had to go through a closing package of legal documents for review. Two or three weeks later, if all was in order, they were approved, and then loans were funded "at the table" when customers arrived. What we call a "table loan" in the mortgage business is a loan that is repaid by periodic payments of principal and interest over the loan term. This results in a declining principal balance and, eventually, repayment of the loan in full.

Commercial banks really did not make residential mortgage loans in the 1980s, but they did buy mortgages from S&Ls for their own portfolios. Mortgage agencies like Fannie Mae and Freddie Mac also bought mortgages from S&Ls for their portfolios and would eventually start to issue their own mortgage securities during that time. Stan immersed himself in the world of mortgages to understand every step of the process.

One benefit gained when using craftsman-like methods to underwrite a loan manually is proficiency in the craft. An individual can understand all the bits and pieces, because they were the one who put them together over a long period of time. Stan and his team acquired an understanding of liens and titles. They learned how to build a credit file, get that file approved by the bank, and take that loan through funding and the close. For Stan, this was a tremendous period of learning and acquiring the highly detailed skills needed to run his growing mortgage business effectively. In simple terms, that meant underwriting loans that the S&Ls and other buyers wanted to own. Stan said:

> When we were able to get up to one hundred transactions a month, we thought we were dancing on air. We were driving in a great deal of income and our business was thriving. All the employees were getting paid and the business was profitable. It had taken us a long time to build up that capability, including hiring and training many good people, but it was well worth it.

One of Stan's great complaints when he began the mortgage business was that he didn't have anybody with five years of experience in mortgage lending. After five years, he didn't have enough people with ten years' experience. He didn't have many people who knew how Stan saw or did things or shared Stan's evolving understanding of the world, which was an important piece of who they were as a company.

Even in those days, Stan continued to focus his approach to building wealth through the prudent use of leverage to make homeownership a reality. This was the key driver for the business. Yet, few people really understood or appreciated the power of that idea. In order to make this vision a reality as a business, Stan developed the understanding and skills in relationship to credit that would allow them to build a really big business in the future. And what they lacked in experience was more than made up for in loyalty. Stan said in an interview:

Not only did I need my employees to be loyal to me, I knew I had to be loyal to them in return. I enjoyed bringing younger people into my business, teaching them and then watching them grow. I enjoyed it when older people came into my business and taught me. And I tried to make sure that everybody who worked with me had a clear role.

We worked hard to build esprit de corps, particularly throughout the earlier days. We had company barbecues. We played ball on weekends. We had parties. We celebrated every victory, and together we mourned every defeat. We enjoyed getting to know each other's families. We knew each other well. We understood that life was filled with challenges. As our children were born and grew and our families took shape, we were all in it together.

Unfortunately, by the late 1980s, interest rates again rose back up into double digits. The favorable conditions that had led to Stan's tremendous growth were ending. There was what we now know as the S&L disaster, when many small lenders went under because they paid more for deposits than they made on loans. S&Ls borrowed short via deposits and lent long via thirty-year mortgages. This was a recipe for disaster. When interest rates increased, the S&Ls were quickly left underwater on fixed rate mortgage loans, leaving many of them insolvent. When interest rates increased, these small, often poorly managed institutions saw their deposit rates rise dramatically.

In an effort to hide the problem, capital standards for S&Ls were debased. The government in effect doubled down and allowed many insolvent S&Ls to continue operating for years, ultimately creating an even bigger mess for the industry to clean up by the end of the decade.

The S&L crisis occurred from 1982 on, when 1,043 out of the 3,234 S&L associations failed over a nine-year period. The Resolution Trust Corporation shuttered 747 institutions in that same period. At the time, the big commercial banks were also a mess because of bad loans to Third World nations and trouble in the oil sector. A bank called Penn Square had failed in 1982, damaging five other large banks in the process and setting in motion a decade of restructuring in Texas real estate and the oil patch.

The failure of Continental Illinois in 1984, then several banks in Texas, and finally Bank of New England in 1990 finished off a difficult decade in the world of American finance. And as mentioned earlier, none of the big commercial banks were really involved in mortgage lending in a significant way. That would change in the 1990s, as commercial banks entered housing finance with fateful consequences a decade later. And Stan Middleman, as a growing player in the world of nonbank mortgage finance, had a front-row seat at the table.

The Importance of People

Stan's business took off during the early 1980s, when interest rates fell from highs of 16 percent into single digits. A few years later, however, when interest rates shot back up through 10 percent and higher, that put the brakes on new mortgage originations, literally in a matter of weeks. As is the case in any cyclical industry, Stan was forced to reduce his head count and lost a lot of good people in the process. By Christmas of 1988, new loan activity had fallen so low that Stan had to serve cold cuts and white bread and a case of beer at the company holiday party.

Stan recalls being heartened to see that a very small group of people still attended the annual celebration, but they all knew that tough times lay ahead. Yet, his core group was committed to continuing to build the business. They believed that there was still meaningful activity to be done and that they could grow from there, which gave Stan confidence in his own leadership and vision. During that sad period, Stan remembers:

> We talked earlier about an idea starting with one person. But to build and grow an idea takes an ever-expanding community of people who share a goal and a vision. At that moment in 1988, when the economy had slowed significantly when the Federal Reserve took interest rates up, things seemed rather gloomy. Yet I saw that we had the true believers, a core team we needed in order to continue to grow. Sometimes people lose their faith when times are tough. Sometimes people who you want to stay decide to leave.
>
> One key member of the team that was with me in those early days was Maria Gallucci, who was responsible for finance even before the creation of Freedom Mortgage. When rates were high in the late 1980s and it was very difficult to get paid or close a loan, Maria juggled the balls in terms of managing our cash flow and kept us alive during some of the darkest days. Sometimes with customers who didn't lock in a fixed rate, we had to put them into adjustable-rate loans. It was quite a challenge to take people who thought they were getting a fixed

rate and then put them in an adjustable-rate loan. Even though it made sense for the consumer, it wasn't the outcome we were hoping for. Just to try to keep the business going, all this extra effort was necessary. That was an extremely difficult time.

In difficult times, often Stan and other business managers in the mortgage industry had to let some good people leave, even though they really wanted them to stay. They just couldn't afford them. Of course, a handful of employees like Maria Gallucci joined the company in the 1980s and have stayed on to eventually become leaders at the firm.

Stan believes that if you're going to be a good leader, you have to believe in yourself and where you're going and then impart that belief to others. You can't lead large groups of people if you're unable to lead small groups of people. That means that you have to be able to deal with people one at a time, look them in the eye, and tell them the hard truth. Sometimes that is not easy.

The S&L crisis put Stan and other mortgage lenders in the unhappy position of having to lay off many of the people whom they personally hired and trained. Stan had built so much camaraderie and team spirit that having to downsize the business was devastating. He had to tell folks that he couldn't afford to pay them.

"We weren't doing as much business as we wanted to do and the economy and mortgage market wouldn't allow us to do more," Stan remembers ruefully. "At the time, other businesses involved in banking and mortgage lending were downsizing as well. The government, ironically but sadly, would hire many experienced people from the mortgage industry to work for the Resolution Trust Corp and resolve the estates of dead Savings & Loans."

The pain caused by this downturn in the mortgage industry was a personal sorrow for Stan. Over the next thirty years, he would get used to dealing with the downside of higher interest rates. These slumps would happen many more times. As we discussed earlier, the interest rate cycle defines much of the reality in the economy. When interest rates come down, they are likely to be followed by interest rates going up. When opportunity seems at its best, there is a problem lurking right around the corner. In the late 1980s, Stan was just starting to pay attention to and learn to identify changes in business cycles, but this huge downturn caught him by surprise and was a very tough lesson.

Managing through the Business Cycle

"There are experiences and conversations you have in life that stay with you," says Stan of that terrible year. "I'll never forget the advice I heard from someone who had seen this all before. I was delivering a huge box of files to Tri-County Savings & Loan Association in Camden, New Jersey. I stopped by the office of George Billings. He was the president of the savings bank, which offered loans throughout South Jersey. We had become friendly over the years of doing business together."

He told Stan: "One thing you need to know is that no matter how good business is going, it's not very long until it's terrible. Our business follows the real estate cycle, which moves every eight or ten years. It's up at one point and it's down at another, and then it comes back. Our job is to make sure we're doing a good job of managing that cycle throughout the life of it."

George Billings ran a small S&L in a really tough neighborhood in Camden, New Jersey, across the Delaware River from Philadelphia. The area once bustled with industry but had already been deteriorating for years. That conversation with Mr. Billings was a major part of Stan's education, both about the cyclical nature of the industry and about how these cycles played out in different areas of the country.

"His words have resonated with me throughout the rest of my career," Stan told me. "This was when the realization came that I had to understand where we were in the economic cycle and pay attention to it."

Stan never forgot this lesson of managing the cycles in the mortgage business, the most cyclical industry of all. Much of his success came from learning to see around the corner as inevitably we see the business cycle change. You know it will change, but the question is, how will it change? What is different this time around on the repeating carousel of risk? But it was also important to understand how the performance of the economy changes over time and in different markets and regions. This idea of regional differences in real estate markets was another important lesson for Stan at this time.

Stan began to understand not only that it was important to watch the economic cycle on a national basis but also that different parts of the country behaved in their own cycles in terms of real estate and credit. As Stan became more focused on following the national economic environment, he noticed that property values did not decline across the country and not all at the same time. Property values fell in the East, yet they remained strong in the Midwest, the Rocky Mountain states, and in the Western states. Stan remembers his realization that the vast American real estate market remained very regional and local as a business and economy:

> As that interest rate change started to take place and business slowed down in the contiguous Eastern states, I watched other companies that did what I did in the West

remain successful and experience tremendous growth. The disease that had stymied our entire business in the Philadelphia area didn't affect mortgage lenders in the other states.

The idea of geographic risk, of being too concentrated in an area, became the first challenge that Stan wanted to learn to manage. At the start, he was a mortgage broker who only conducted business in one or two states. As time went on, his firm began working in additional states under separate companies. Dealing with the practical issues of expanding into new territory, Stan came to understand the need for the business to have a national orientation. This was both to avoid geographic risks and to benefit when some areas were relatively strong. This was a monumental epiphany, which had enormous ramifications for Stan's trajectory as the owner of a growing mortgage business.

In those last days of the decade, many lenders were focused on their local area, covering a few states or sometimes only a single state. This meant that the lender had a concentration in a given area in terms of credit and also had operational risk. Firms with little or no regional diversification were vulnerable to a major economic event or natural catastrophe. And as the years went on, the lesson of following the differences in each region would enable Stan to avoid risk and seize opportunities that we'll discuss later in the book.

When Stan realized this fact, that geographic risks and opportunities were quite different, suddenly he realized that the business needed to change.

"We decided in the late 1980s that we'd have to find a way to avoid falling victim to localized issues in the real estate market, whether it was defaults or loan prepayments. We also needed to start learning about the world of mortgage servicing rights or MSRs."

Stan was starting to think strategically about the rate at which mortgage loans repaid over a period of years, particularly in different parts of the country. In order to do this, he needed to become a national mortgage banking company. Stan made the conscious decision to take the next step and start Freedom Mortgage.

MORTGAGE BANKER

When Stan started Freedom Mortgage in 1990, he had a couple of specific motivations and objectives in making the change. He wanted to become a mortgage banker rather than merely a loan broker. Stan also felt that could better handle the state compliance for lenders in one centralized firm rather than in separate businesses, which he had set up in each state under United Financial.

Using "Freedom" as part of the name reflected Stan's worldview that the best mortgage is no mortgage at all. He wanted a name that was an idea: that Freedom Mortgage would help its customers eventually become free of a mortgage. He saw a mortgage as a compromise that initially restricted consumer freedom because of the cost but could also become a very important part of a consumer's journey to financial security.

"Freedom Mortgage was a name that brought together my local pride in the city where our town and my business life were born and also my business philosophy," Stan recalls. "Freedom Mortgage was more than a place or a company, it was about an idea I first developed selling annuities which was to help our customers build wealth and achieve financial freedom. I saw mortgages as a burden and I wanted to help people become free of their mortgages."

In the 1990s, most Americans still reflected the Depression mentality that debt was bad. In contrast to the more liberal social perspectives of the 2000s, people avoided defaulting on their debts because of the social stigma involved. The personal finance companies of that era would think nothing of sending out a debt collector when a loan became delinquent. In fact, the people who made consumer loans oftentimes had to collect bad debts, one way that finance companies like HFC Associates or even banks such as Manufacturers Hannover made sure that their loan officers made good loans.

Originally, Stan wanted to use the name "liberty" for his business, but it was not available. Along with the emergence of a name that would lend itself to a national operation, which was his aspiration, Freedom Mortgage allowed Stan to meet the next goal for the business in the context of a larger ambition to be a national player in home mortgages. Between 1985 and 1990, Stan had run his business as a series of companies located in different states. Each jurisdiction had its own rules and licensing requirements. Stan wanted to make sure that a problem in one office, which might have a single manager and a dozen salespeople, would not impact the other offices.

Over time, however, as the business grew in size and complexity, Stan came to realize that he needed to centralize things like operations, finance, and compliance with state laws governing the mortgage business. By this time, his firm was doing business in five states. As he increased his proficiency as a manager, Stan came to understand that he needed to take the next step and form a single firm.

"We took the decision to pull everyone together, invest in training and compliance, and see if we could not manage compliance risk more efficiently," Stan recalls. "Little did I know that that was really just licensing! I had taken the originators exam in New Jersey. A regulator from the New Jersey Department of Banking came to visit and he was curious about our operation. They really did not have many nonbank mortgage firms operating in those days. All of the regulators were very helpful and we all learned a lot. The state regulators mentored me in bank rules and regulations at a crucial time for us."

When Stan founded Freedom Mortgage in New Jersey in 1990, the firm obtained a license as a mortgage banker. New Jersey had some of the toughest laws in the United States governing the mortgage business, which was an extension of the regulation of banks. Stan got to know the regulators who were responsible for his new business and spent a lot of time learning all the compliance and reporting requirements for mortgage bankers. The regulators were very helpful, in part because there were still so few independent mortgage bankers in a home loan market dominated by commercial banks.

Stan Middleman entered the world of consumer lending at a time when the US economy was still recovering from the Great Depression and World War II, when large banks dominated all aspects of finance. While millions of words have been said and written about the subprime mortgage crisis of 2008, many people still don't understand that it was largely commercial banks that widely introduced subprime mortgage loans as a product to the US housing market. Stan was a witness to this momentous change in the world of mortgage lending.

S&Ls, also known as "thrifts," were the main providers of conventional residential mortgage loans in the United States after the Great Depression. With the creation of Fannie Mae in 1938, the government created a market for thirty-year fixed rate mortgages. The S&Ls were the dominant providers of mortgage credit for decades afterward. But these thinly capitalized near-banks were decimated in the 1980s, when Federal Reserve Board chairman Paul Volcker lifted interest rates to double digits to fight inflation.

Even when Stan was first getting started in the mortgage business, big banks still dominated the financing of the US economy. The big state-chartered banks and the S&Ls lent on commercial property and residential credits. National banks could not even lend on real estate until well after World War II but would soon become a significant factor in the world of mortgage finance for independent players, such as Stan's Freedom Mortgage. The buyers of the loans originated by mortgage banking firms, usually banks, effectively governed the mortgage market.

Only with the development of a secondary market for mortgage loans in the 1970s, when Ginnie Mae sold the first mortgage securities to investors, and we saw the rise of nonbank finance, did credit slowly become more widely available for consumers. Technology and the marketplace combined to create not only enormous opportunity but also some enormous risk from the Federal Reserve Board when it came to the ebb and flow of interest rates and employment.

As a young mortgage banker operating in the Philadelphia market, Stan Middleman had a front-row seat, as the market for subprime mortgages was born. New businesses such as Freedom Mortgage rode a demographic wave of pent-up demand for homes and also greater prosperity that slowly increased during this period. "A bubble formed in the housing markets as home prices across the country increased each year from the mid-1990s to 2006, moving out of line with fundamentals like household income," Brookings Institution wrote of that time.[10]

For many independent mortgage bankers active during that period, the early years were slow but picked up steam depending upon movements in interest rates. It was the arrival of the larger banks during the time that changed the size and breadth of the mortgage market forever. In fact, it was neither S&Ls nor nonbank mortgage firms but Citibank N.A. that actually offered one of the first subprime, "no-doc" mortgages in the US mortgage market.

A "no-doc" mortgage was a loan with little to no documentation about the borrower or their income, a risky product that would cause big problems two decades later. Under CEO John Reed, Citibank began a journey of innovation into new areas of consumer financial services, often as the trailblazer of the industry. Citibank took risks that many other banks would not even consider. Simply stated, Citibank adopted the credit underwriting processes of a nonbank finance company.

The traditional method used by lenders to assess the credit worthiness of an individual, based on the three C's of credit (capacity, character, and collateral),[11] was cast off by Citibank under Reed in order to win new business. By discarding the traditional rules of credit, Citibank hoped to create a new market for subprime consumer finance. John Reed wrote way back in 1976, while Stan was still in college in Philadelphia:

10   Martin Neil Baily, Robert E. Litan, and Matthew S. Johnson, "The Origins of the Financial Crisis," Brookings Institution, Fixing Finance no. 3, November 2008, https://www.brookings.edu/wp-content/uploads/2016/06/11_origins_crisis_baily_litan.pdf.

11   "The Three C's of Credit," Federal Reserve Bank of St. Louis, accessed August 2023, https://www.stlouisfed.org/education/making-personal-finance-decisions-curriculum-unit/three-cs-of-credit.

> We are creating something new. I refer to a fundamentally
> new business starting with a dedication to the consumer,
> and to the proposition that we can offer a set of services
> that will substantially satisfy a family's financial needs
> under terms and conditions that will earn the sharehold-
> ers an adequate profit while creating a healthy, positive
> and straightforward relationship with the customer.

In the year that Stan graduated from Temple University, Citibank issued a bank credit card globally, Citicard, and began to place ATMs in all of its branches. Over the next decade, Citibank would become the largest credit card issuer in the world, operating in more than ninety countries. A decade later, Citibank entered the residential mortgage market in a big way with a product they called the "Mortgage Power" program. This new product was offered to customers around the world, not just in the US mortgage market, and with disastrous results for Citibank.

Mortgage Power was a risky type of loan, a no-doc, no-income verification credit product of the type that would figure significantly in the 2008 financial crisis. The marketing message from Citibank was that the Mortgage Power product was designed to fit the needs of the self-employed and otherwise underserved people who generally could never qualify for a mortgage at a bank. Today, mainstream lenders will easily accept and fund a bank statement loan, but in the mid-1980s, this was a very new territory for Citibank and the banking industry.

By creating a new market for people that could not traditionally access bank loans, Citibank gradually replaced the larger (and failed) S&Ls as the wholesale buyer of residential mortgages from brokers like Stan. The entry of Citibank and other banks such as Norwest into this still-small secondary marketplace for loans coincided with the growth and development of Freedom Mortgage and many other private mortgage firms in the early 1990s.

Even as Stan Middleman built Freedom Mortgage, Citibank revolutionized subprime mortgage processing. The bankers at Citibank truly only required a borrower to fog a mirror to get a loan approval. Commercial loans were a big source of losses to US banks in the recession years of the early 1980s, but by the 1990s, Citibank's residential mortgage business was also hemorrhaging red ink. In the year Freedom Mortgage opened its doors for business, Citibank's bad mortgage loans rose to almost 4 percent of total loans, a staggering financial loss for a large bank at that time.[12]

The Takeout Buyer

For Stan and many other mortgage bankers operating in the 1990s, selling loans to larger banks such as Citibank was the path of least resistance in the secondary loan market. Citibank would buy loans from smaller lenders, close the mortgage, and then issue securities guaranteed by one of the housing agencies. This all sounded great, but the banks like Citibank also acquired a lot of risk in the process of buying and selling mortgages. Stan recounted those days in a 2020 interview:

> Citibank had processors to handle the documentation, so all we had to do was start the application process and schedule the closing. We did the disclosure on the loan and then shipped the documents off to Citibank. These were no-income, no-asset loans. Citibank did whatever else they did, which was not much—drew the docs and

---

12 Michael Quint, "Mortgage Woes Rise at Citicorp," *The New York Times*, November 21, 1990, https://www.nytimes.com/1990/11/21/business/mortgage-woes-rise-at-citicorp.html.

closed the loan. In this way, Citibank became among the top aggregators in the mortgage industry in the 1980s and early 1990s. At the time, I was not very worldly or well-connected in the mortgage industry, but everybody I knew in mortgages in New Jersey was selling loans to Citibank. Why would you do them any other way?

The Citibank no-doc, subprime loan product reported double-digit losses to federal regulators during that period.[13] In simple terms, Citibank got absolutely crushed financially for acting as the "takeout" investor or buyer of subprime residential mortgages made by other lenders. In 2000, one study calculated, nearly three of every four mortgages originated within Citigroup's lending empire were made by other lenders—nearly 180,000 loans out of a total of 240,000-plus mortgages for the year.[14]

After what was then known as Citicorp stumbled financially in the early 1990s, the bank left the mortgage industry for most of the decade until after the 1998 merger with Travelers. Yet, even after taking a beating financially in the 1990s, Citibank and other large bank lenders all eventually returned to mortgage lending because of the enormous volumes involved. They just could not resist the huge profit opportunity in residential lending, especially when interest rates were low, the economy was riding high, and credit concerns faded from memory.

In the beginning of Stan's career, mortgage lending was largely a nonbank market. National banks generally avoided consumer lending and especially residential mortgages. Thrifts and large state-chartered banks dominated mortgage lending. The commercial bankers of

---

13   Dean Starkman, "Understanding Citi Losses in Its Predatory Roots," *Columbia Journal Review,* October 15, 2009, https://archives.cjr.org/the_audit/understanding_citigroups_losse.php.

14   Ibid.

that era were very conservative people who wore suits and took no risk. Most mainstream banks generally only loaned on collateral and wanted your deposits to fund the loan. The bankers went to the office around 9:30 in the morning and were headed home or to the golf course by four o'clock in the afternoon.

Stockbrokers, investment bankers, and consumer finance people were a distinct social segment from the commercial bankers. Mortgage bankers like Stan Middleman worked eighty-hour weeks. Consumer lenders working at nonbank firms were compensated via commissions, a different breed who focused on sales rather than credit. But only the consumer lenders that pay attention to credit and overall production quality, Stan Middleman quickly learned, survive the inevitable ebb and flow of the economy and interest rates.

In the decade after Stan graduated from Temple University in the spring of 1976, home mortgages already had begun the migration from a sleepy, parochial business to being a national market impacted by global events only a decade later. When Stan Middleman established Freedom Mortgage fifteen years later, he started that journey just as the S&L crisis hobbled the US economy.

Stan's experience watching the S&L crisis play out convinced him that his firm needed to expand its geographic focus to include the entire country, not just to grow revenue but also to manage risk. Interest rates and the dollar were being buffeted by global forces outside of the traditional domestic focus of most people. Being a national mortgage firm with the ability to buy loans in different markets was a hedge against these fluctuations as well as a bigger market opportunity for Stan and his growing team.

One of the members of Stan's early team at Freedom Mortgage was Dan Hefferon, who worked as a manager of a couple of large restaurants and was very well organized. He joined Freedom Mortgage in the early 1990s and quickly learned the mortgage business. Over time, Dan became a key manager at Freedom Mortgage and remained with the firm until he retired at the end of 2023.

"Dan was very bright and started as a salesman at Freedom Mortgage," remembers Stan. "Over his first decade he evolved into more of an administrative role. He worked more in the mortgage finance side of the business dealing with our bank lenders. Dan was a stable and steadying force who helped to counterbalance some of the energy in a business built on sales. Along with many other people in that period, Dan helped to build Freedom Mortgage into an enduring business."

Even with the development into a national franchise in addition to other changes that were made to the Freedom Mortgage model, Stan and his team frequently felt stymied by the vagaries of changes in interest rates and the economy. When interest rates went up and sales fell, Stan had to consolidate the business and reduce head count quickly just in order to survive. Being held hostage by interest rates is the world of the small independent mortgage banker, builder, or real estate agent.

There were some thin years in the 1990s for lenders, many of which had to downsize in a significant fashion in order to survive in times of high interest rates and low lending volumes. Bank credit would often disappear, sometimes without notice. Freedom Mortgage and other lenders had to cut volumes and focus on loans that they could sell at a profit. A low interest rate environment meant expansion, but rising interest rates forced mortgage lenders to get back to the core values of business viability or risk failure. Rising rates meant more competition for fewer good loans and thus tighter profit margins.

"Even though we were able to sell, and had more customers to see to than ever before, we had to rethink the cyclical risks constantly," Stan recalls of that period. "We needed to understand the hazards that faced us so that we wouldn't have to go backward just in order to stay alive. As interest rates rose, it became more and more difficult to sell mortgages, because there's less mortgages to be sold."

While lenders set the coupons on each loan they make, market interest rates ultimately set the price of mortgage credit. When interest rates rise, the refinance opportunities go away, and all that's left are a few purchase mortgages. Early on, Stan's business was really anchored in refinancing existing mortgages rather than creating new mortgages for new home purchases. Stan had to constantly reinvent Freedom Mortgage to be able to capture purchase money mortgages rather than take advantage of refinancing opportunities when interest rates fell. The following advertisement came from the *Philadelphia Inquirer* in July 1992:

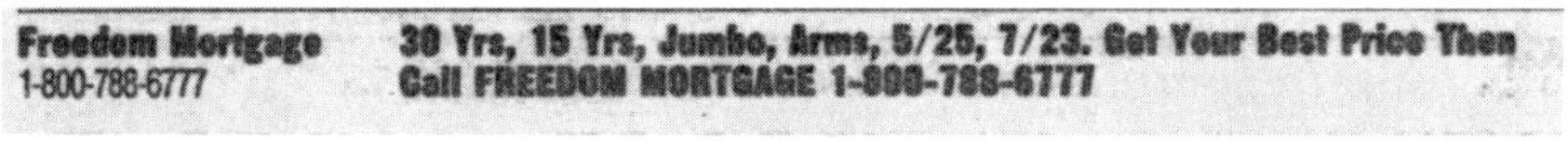

Freedom Mortgage   30 Yrs, 15 Yrs, Jumbo, Arms, 5/25, 7/23. Get Your Best Price Then
1-800-788-6777   Call FREEDOM MORTGAGE 1-800-788-6777

Figure 6.1.

In order to navigate through the lean years of Freedom Mortgage's first decade, Stan rebuilt the organization over and over, an experience many lenders today understand all too well. They needed to acquire new and different skills to perform the key tasks involved to make and sell a loan. They had to get better at these tasks to lend at acceptable price levels to create profitability. The adoption of automated statistical scoring and underwriting for mortgages, for example, was a big factor after 1995, when the industry applied the tools from credit cards and auto lending to approving mortgages.

Adopting new techniques and technologies was an ever-present challenge for Stan, but it was also an exciting opportunity for him to create opportunities for homeownership at a time when getting a mortgage was difficult. It is some testament to the efforts of Freedom

Mortgage and other independent mortgage bankers that home loans granted to low-income and minority Americans rose sharply during the 1990s.[15] Unlike banks, which basically wait for demand to find them, Stan's company needed to actively expand its revenue and product universe to reach out to new markets. And swings in interest rates were not the only challenge.

As Freedom Mortgage went through a tough downsizing in the middle of the decade, a new business model took shape where anticipating changes related to interest rates and technology—that is, seeing around corners—and adjusting accordingly became the core skill set for Stan and his senior managers. Ever since that first decade in operation, in fact, one of the biggest challenges facing mortgage bankers has been which new technology to adopt.

Amid the growing uncertainty about interest rates and the economy during that period, Stan and his team needed to work even harder than before to ensure stable profits and better manage the ebb and flow of the economic cycle, in terms of both demand for loans and mortgage defaults. This meant that Freedom Mortgage had to go from being merely a mortgage broker, which originated and sold loans to S&Ls and commercial banks, to being a full-blown mortgage bank. That meant that Freedom Mortgage originated mortgages in its own name, using various sources of financing, mostly the larger commercial banks.

In that first decade, Freedom Mortgage began to retain the servicing rights on some loans, an important part of the strategy of managing and taking prudent advantage of moves in interest rates to build long-term profitability. MSRs represent the contractual right of a lender to receive monthly fees for servicing your mortgage. When

---

15   Robert A. Rosenblatt, "Home Loans to Poor Rose in '90s," Los Angeles Times, April 20, 2020, https://www.latimes.com/archives/la-xpm-2000-apr-20-fi-21554-story.html.

interest rates rise and few people are refinancing their mortgage or buying a new home, the value of MSRs rises. In technical terms, we say that MSRs have negative duration while a loan or a bond has a positive duration.[16]

"After we won our approval as an agency lender with Freddie Mac, we got our first bank warehouse line from GE Capital Corp," Stan remembers with pride. "We started funding some loans in our own name, although we continued to be primarily a correspondent lender. Whereas in the past we originated a loan for another bank, now we could originate and close the loan, and then sell the loan into a variety of markets. We also began to think and learn about mortgage servicing, both as a business and also as a way to create and manage a valuable financial asset that was largely the preserve of the big banks."

We've discussed how the mortgage lending business is very sensitive to interest rates, in terms of the pricing of both new and existing loans. But interest rates also impact the value of the *mortgage servicing portfolios*, which these loans represent. A loan in a Ginnie Mae mortgage pool pays the servicer of the loan roughly one-third of 1 percent of the unpaid principal balance of the mortgage each year to cover the cost of servicing. How long that loan remains in the servicing portfolio determines the value of the mortgage servicing investment. And how interest rates rise and fall determines how fast a mortgage pays off, when

---

16   Boyce (2010) notes that an MSR is the present value of the interest only (IO) cash flow stream that exists between the mortgage note rate and bond coupon, net of GSE guarantee fees, and servicing costs. An MSR is a source of cheap, negative duration for lenders and investors in these assets. Specifically, MSRs are IOs that are negatively convex. And significantly for investors, MSRs are a "tax deferred asset" and a "non-cash asset." Corporate taxes are only paid on the net income realized from the cash flow stream of the MSR net of any loan servicing expense and amortization. Generally accepted accounting principles (GAAP) recognize the noncash gain from mortgage origination, which today is a small fraction of the value of the capitalized MSR. See also: Richard Christopher Whalen, "Increasing Capital & Liquidity for GNMA Mortgage Servicing Rights," June 19, 2018, https://ssrn.com/abstract=3176147.

a consumer buys another house or refinances an existing mortgage. As interest rates rise, fewer borrowers voluntarily pay off their loans, and thus, the mortgage servicing portfolio increases in value.

Rising mortgage rates loomed large over the mortgage finance industry as lending volumes fell and the value of mortgage servicing income soared. From 1993 to 1994, for example, interest rates basically doubled. Orange County defaulted on its debts because of derivatives it had purchased from Deutsche Bank. These events illustrated the risks and rewards that came with the interest rate cycle. But the increased value of MSRs in a rising interest rate environment became a valuable asset for Stan and Freedom Mortgage. Income from loans and servicing rights he had retained during good times helped the firm to survive when interest rates rose and lending volumes fell.

"Over the years, I spent many hours talking to mortgage bankers who bought and sold servicing portfolios to understand this obscure but very profitable part of the business," Stan reflects about mortgage servicing assets. "Simply stated, the right to receive servicing fees—known as a mortgage servicing right or MSR—goes up in value when interest rates rise. It is the only naturally occurring negative duration asset in the world of finance. Also, the MSR is really not a true *intangible asset* since it represents the right to receive significant cash flows. And most important and most valuable, the MSR represents your relationship with the consumer."

Loans and fixed income securities, such as bonds, generally have positive *duration*. Duration is a fancy term for how long it takes for you as an investor to receive your money back. Because of the negative duration of servicing assets, however, MSRs are actually a great financial and economic hedge for a residential loan portfolio. Why? Because as we noted earlier, when interest rates rise, people are less likely to move or seek new loans, either to purchase a home or refinance. The length of time people will stay in their homes—and the duration of the MSR—extends in time, so the *net present value* of the servicing income from the MSR is greater.

Ultimately, interest rates and the net present value of the servicing income determine much of the value of the mortgage loan and related servicing assets. Higher rates make a pool of existing mortgages very stable and thus more attractive to a mortgage bank or a financial investor. Rising interest rates make it less likely that a mortgage will *prepay* or be repaid early, making the *average life* of the pool of mortgages longer in terms of time the loans are outstanding. A longer average life for the pool of mortgages makes the fees earned each month for servicing the loans more valuable over time. Congratulations, now you understand the basics of mortgage banking!

The first agency approval obtained by Freedom Mortgage came from Freddie Mac in the early 1990s. The people at Freddie Mac were a little more user-friendly than Fannie, but Freedom Mortgage got approved by Fannie Mae shortly thereafter. Freedom Mortgage was still primarily a correspondent lender, buying loans from other lenders, but Stan also started to fund loans to retain in portfolio and thereby build assets for the company. The early focus on retaining earnings and investing excess cash into assets, such as loans and mortgage servicing, would become a key part of Freedom Mortgage's success.

Like everyone else making mortgage loans in the mid-Atlantic states during the early 1990s, Stan did a lot of business with Citibank, Norwest Bank, Countrywide, and a variety of other institutions. As many remaining S&Ls were closed or forced to raise capital, the commercial banks moved into residential mortgages. And gradually, after those lean years in the mid-1990s, when interest rates began to fall again near the end of the decade, business improved dramatically. Deregulation allowed nationwide banking, enabling well-funded lenders, such as GMAC, Countrywide, and Norwest, to take on a bigger leadership role in the industry, buying loans originated by independent correspondent firms. Stan talked about his role in those years:

"As a correspondent lender, we generally conformed the loans we did for other lenders to their specifications. Our attitude was that it was their money so we'd do it their way. We developed all of our processes around their demands. But some commercial banks in the wholesale mortgage business had better lending standards than others."

Over time, the processes Freedom Mortgage used for underwriting home loans for different lenders around the country became relatively homogenized. A conventional loan eligible for Fannie Mae or Freddie Mac, for example, was largely fungible between different lenders. Even today, conventional loans are not entirely fungible between Fannie Mae and Freddie Mac, but in those days, the loan specifications were reasonably close.

In the early 1990s, it took months to get a loan ready for submission to the bank, and then maybe half would get approved, Stan recalls. It was hard to get a loan in those days. It was hard to verify income in those days. Mortgage banks were at a disadvantage to the banks because, for a lot of borrowers with more conventional financial histories, their first choice was the local bank. Home mortgage was a very parochial business, and a lot of people preferred to do business with their local realtor and bank than an independent mortgage banker.

Stan almost immediately saw benefits from changing his business model from a regional lender to a national lender. Markets and banks in the east encountered difficulties first, and then the problems moved west. But by the time lenders in the west were really in trouble, banks in the east were starting to get healthy again. Property values began to recover in the east. Watching this process, Stan learned an important corollary to the rule of following interest rates, namely, the regional and even local nature of real estate markets and mortgage credit trends.

Maintaining geographic diversity in the residential mortgage business was an important lesson for Stan and his team. The problems the firm experienced in the east, for example, were largely over by the time the cycle moved to the west. And by the time they were starting to see new problems or trends in the east, the western markets had largely healed. If real estate is about "location, location, location" to use the old adage, then different markets around the country also behave differently.

After three decades in the mortgage business, Stan saw his firm impacted first by local events, then regional, and eventually by national and even worldwide events. Since Stan first entered the world of consumer finance, the speed of information flow has changed mortgage lending and other services from being a localized business to becoming a business closely connected to the financial markets. There was also a trend toward greater specialization by lenders, as the distinction between banks and independent mortgage banks in the secondary market began to blur. Stan talked about the early days in a 2021 interview:

> "The world really didn't matter to a mortgage lender in Philadelphia in the 1980s. Something that happened in Chicago didn't matter on the east coast. Stuff that happened on the west coast really didn't matter in Chicago. But when we watched the sudden changes that occurred, being a national firm made a huge difference. We watched the economy go into recession in the early 1990s, followed by a drop in interest rates, from over 8 percent for Fed funds in 1990 to just over 3 percent by 1993. We saw a major rebound that drove our business to the next level.

And during this time, we became very focused on learning about the world of mortgage banking as opposed to merely being a loan broker selling warm leads. By 1994, however, the spike in interest rates engineered by the Fed sent many people in the industry scrambling to survive."

Another big challenge for Stan in that time was finding people with the knowledge and the skills to join a sales-driven organization. Muses Stan:

"There were not that many independent mortgage companies twenty-five years ago. We did not have a big field of personnel from which to hire people, so finding the right individuals to broaden our capabilities in capital markets and mortgage servicing took a great deal of time. I did not yet have the capital to buy mortgage servicing portfolios as we do today, but we wanted to understand how the market valued mortgages. We worked to learn all of the pieces of the world of mortgage finance."

As Freedom Mortgage began to accumulate loans and servicing assets for the firm's portfolio, Stan quickly found that he got better execution—industry slang for making money when you sell a loan into the bond market—by holding the assets back for a period and then selling them at a different time—sometimes years later. This experience dovetailed with Stan's interest in buying and holding loans and servicing assets as investments.

Stan initially kept all the loans he made in the early 1990s, along with the servicing. Later, Stan sold the servicing when interest rates rose, and the MSR valuations likewise increased during a volatile period. Stan retained significantly more production later in the decade and, as we discuss later in this book, sold those assets for a big profit near the end of the decade, as rates were slowly starting to rise. As interest rates rose toward the end of the decade, Stan generated a lot of new capital in cash for Freedom Mortgage by selling MSRs to investors.

The moral of the story based upon the success enjoyed by Stan Middleman and Freedom Mortgage in the MSR market: buy low and sell high. You originate the loans when interest rates are low and mortgage servicing is worth little, and then sell the MSRs later at a much higher price as rates rise. Now you understand mortgage servicing assets! And in a very simplistic sense, this is precisely how Stan learned about the business of making and investing in mortgage assets.

"Although some analysts think that the high prices paid for MSRs in the six- and seven-times annual cash flow multiple territory during 2018 were extraordinary, in fact we've seen similar price action in past interest rate cycles," Stan notes with some satisfaction. "To sell conforming loan MSRs at a seven multiple to annual cash flow in the late 1990s was not a bad return in my book."

Stan notes that the true economic value of mortgage servicing assets is probably closer to three to four times the annual servicing cash flow; thus, the values seen in the 1990s and more recently are even more remarkable. Ultimately, though, the price of loans and mortgage servicing are a function of interest rates, which are controlled by the Fed. Yet, it is important to note that Freedom Mortgage made a cash profit acquiring the loans and related MSRs in that era and essentially got the servicing for free or at little cost. Even though it was a difficult decade for lenders, Stan's growing understanding of the value of servicing as an investment allowed him to profit handsomely.

The value of homes continued to rise slowly during Freedom Mortgage's first decade, a gradual rebound from the sharp downward correction in home prices a decade before that gave rise to the Resolution Trust Corporation that cleaned up the S&Ls. The optimism and market hype visible with the dot-com explosion and the confidence about the economy also boosted the value of mortgage assets. The changes due to technology were a big part of the general optimism of the time, but this rising confidence would set the stage for the boom and bust a decade later. But at the time, lenders were more concerned about making more loans than worrying about a future downturn.

"People prepared their own letters, things moved faster," Stan says of improvements in technology during that time. "We had typewriters with memory! We got loan documents in weeks instead of months. Faxes were becoming a big part of the process. We could print documents ourselves. We could do disclosure in an automated fashion. The changes occurring throughout all business but especially the mortgage lending world were truly revolutionary."

Then Things Change

Just as his business was undergoing enormous change, so too Stan's personal life underwent a big transformation. First and foremost, the focus changed from Stan and his career goals to being a husband and a father. He remembers: "The fact that Ros and I had children made me focus on both business goals and personal goals in a very different way. The personal responsibilities of being a father and a husband became paramount."

Yet, even as Stan took on the role of a father, his strategy of constant improvement in his professional life also remained a core ethic for him. When Stan thinks of improvement, it is part of a larger idea we can call living a purposeful life. According to Stan, you need to constantly spend time thinking: What is the next thing you can do? What's my next goal or achievement?

Having children made Stan work even harder and also reset his goals. One goal was to build a comfortable life and feed his family and, most important, make sure that the family was secure. That goal became a tremendous driving force for Stan as he went from being a young man to a young father. But he also had a larger family at Freedom Mortgage, hundreds of employees who depended upon Stan and the company for their livelihood.

Between the mid-1980s and the mid-1990s, Stan learned that a lot of constraints and limitations existed that were put in his path by outside factors. Because of what was happening to the mortgage industry at the time, Stan spent a lot of time learning about economic cycles. Rising interest rates were changing the competitive dynamic in the mortgage world. He learned that there were things that were beyond his control. Freedom Mortgage had to prepare to be able to manage the outcomes of the business through those cycles. He didn't want the cycles to control his actions and leave him not in control of his firm's destiny.

"From the time that I was forty in the mid-1990s to the time that I reached fifty a couple years before the financial crisis in 2008, I was focused on creating an outcome and an income personally that would allow me to overcome any economic cycles," he says. "I focused on overcoming one risk after another in our business."

As he went through life, Stan faced several critical junctures where he had to adjust his view, his vision, all the while understanding the larger picture of trying to secure a future for himself and his family. Like all managers, Stan had to help the members of the team realize their dreams in terms of careers and their bigger goals of securing a better life for themselves and *their* families. That responsibility for the larger Freedom Mortgage family became a driving force in doing the same thing for himself and his family. It remains so today, Stan believes, because if you're not sensitive and aware not only of yourself but also to those around you, your ability to achieve becomes dramatically limited.

Freedom Mortgage's longtime employee and senior executive vice president Maria Gallucci often says of those difficult days: "We made a decision that we were not going to go backward. We were always going to go forward."

For Stan, going forward meant first and foremost caring for and protecting members of the team whenever the markets turned. Maria Gallucci has been a key member of Stan's senior management team who continues to help guide the organization through good and bad times.

"Maria joined our team in the 1980s, even before we started Freedom Mortgage," he recalls with pride. "She rose through the ranks to become our Corporate Secretary and Senior EVP, with particular responsibility for funding and closings. Maria has watched our money for more than thirty years."

The downsizing that was forced upon Freedom Mortgage and other lenders during the latter years of the 1990s reinforced Stan's belief that "seeing around corners" requires constant effort and a willingness to change. When we think about changes and phases in life, Stan believes that as you age, you evolve, and as you evolve, you need to constantly reinvent yourself. You must constantly be looking forward and the future must be central to your thinking. You take all of these things, you fight and scrape and struggle, to turn them into something real so that when you are accomplished, you can then teach to others.

Yet, you never let that be the end game, Stan believes. What you've done must never become a substitute for what you're doing next. What you've done must pale in comparison to the importance of what you're about to do. To paraphrase Henry Ford, the only history that matters is the history we make today.

"It was very hard in the beginning when Stan started the mortgage company," recalls Ros Middleman.

> There were a lot of ups and downs. There were times when there was no money coming in. We didn't know how we were going to pay bills. And it's amazing to me his persistence in just wanting to succeed. Stan somehow was able to do that and sustain it all these years. Dozens of Freedom Mortgage employees have been there for over twenty years or more. And I think that tells you a lot about Stan as a person. He cares about them, and he listens to them. And at this point in his life, Stan wants to leave a legacy for our kids and our grandkids and for future generations.

Success Is about Consistency

One of the things Stan tells his children and his colleagues at Freedom Mortgage is that success is cumulative. Success is piling up accomplishments, some big, some small, one on top of another. Focusing on immediate goals and accomplishments drives in the results to create an enduring accomplishment and a long-term outcome. When Stan thinks about success personally or in business, he's thinking about success over time and how we turn our short-term victories into a way of life over a lifetime. The mortgage business or any business, after all, is really about managing risk, about seeing around corners, over many months and years.

"At any point in time you can feel rich, or you can feel broke," argues Stan. "These are temporary conditions. They're how things are at the moment. There are two other words: poor and wealthy. Those words are ways of life. They're not a temporary condition or a momentary condition. I grew up relatively poor. Now I'm relatively wealthy."

When Stan says that he believes that wealthy or poor are ways of life, it's not to say that those ways of life can't change or end. However, change is a process that takes a consistent approach. It takes a series of failures or just inaction to become poor. And whether it was your fault or somebody else's fault, something happened that led you to that place. Or something didn't happen that led you to that place.

"Same thing with wealth," Stan argues. "You can temporarily be rich or be broke, both of which are emblematic of achievement and failure in the short run."

Stan argues that we should think of that choice, wealthy or poor, as we set and adjust our goals throughout our lives. Do you choose to be wealthy? Or do you choose to be apathetic and just get by?

Most people prefer to think about the things that we control that lead us to a place where we can create real wealth over a long period of time and make that success a way of life. That enduring success feeds into more of a feeling of accomplishment. Success feels far different from the feeling of being poor and having things go wrong and then continue to go wrong, creating the "helplessness of hopelessness." Because the more things that go wrong for you, Stan contends, the tendency is to believe things will continue to go against you.

Where does this path to success begin? Where does this direction take hold in a professional life? That path, Stan argues, starts by believing in yourself. Success is where hard work and opportunity meet. And the outcome is given by your ability and experience to prepare to take advantage of that opportunity when it's there. This crossroads is an important one.

There's a place in everyone's life where they choose. "Am I going to be successful? Am I going to get by? Or am I going to be poor?" Success or failure really comes from decisions in the moment. Your approach to life must be that you're interested in success. Stan understands the nature of success is cumulative.

"I like to see people on the job for a long time, to watch them build a series of achievements that drive accomplishments that lead to a big pile of wins that lead to success," Stan reflects on his years at Freedom Mortgage. "There is nothing more satisfying than seeing a colleague grow and achieve success in your organization. That success is the reward for cumulative achievement. How? You must wake up every morning and be determined to be better. One of the great misnomers in the world is striving to be the best. And the reason that's a misnomer is that like rich or broke, it's a temporary state."

You can never be your best all the time, or then it wouldn't be your best, Stan argues. If you did it all the time, it wouldn't be your best; it would just be ordinary. What you need to do is consistently improve. Your sole focus should be on getting better. Ask yourself, "How do I build myself into a better person? How do I acquire new knowledge? How do I build the skills that let me achieve more?"

The answer, Stan believes, is by raising the floor and doing something that may be your best and then turning that best into normal—and making sure that you're constantly improving and striving to get better. What does that have to do with fear? Well, if you're focused on consistently getting better, fear is a tremendous inconvenience. That's the moment of inspiration, Stan recalls of his early experiences in business, the moment of embracing success. When you discard fear and embrace success and constant improvement as your path, you cannot help but succeed. You define your attitude based upon what's happening now. You have to address the circumstances, you have to deal with issues, but you can't spend all your time worrying about them and not dealing with them.

"There can be catastrophes in everyone's life and real setbacks and real hardships," Stan says. "But if you're fortunate to be able to deal with adversity, with the physical and emotional and mental issues that confront you, then you can succeed. And then it just becomes a choice. You make the choice that you're going to become a better and better you. Now sometimes you have to start over. Sometimes you have to embrace your failure and rebuild. Sometimes you're taking ten steps backward to get that first step forward on the eleventh. But it's all about constant improvement."

To achieve success, Stan believes, you need to accumulate victories; you need to amass accomplishments. Gaining experience and knowledge builds confidence. The more confidence you have, the more you can achieve. The more you believe in you, the easier it is to believe in you. The harder you work and the more you understand what you've done, it's easier to understand how much more you have to do. You have to believe in yourself, and you have to get better every day, because without confidence and self-belief, you're left only with fear and no way to overcome it. Confidence, consistency, and continuous improvement are the antidotes to fear.

"More than anything else," Stan recalls, "I wanted them to appreciate that the road to success is paved with failures and near-misses, but that consistency in your approach will always yield good results."

Stan worked hard to convey these ideas about focus and consistency to his children and his extended family at Freedom Mortgage. More than anything, he wanted to see his kids prepared to go forward in life and become active, important contributors to their society without preventing them from enjoying their childhood. This meant introducing some of his personal habits in terms of planning and thinking about the future and talking to them about risks and opportunities in business and in life.

But Stan was not only a good teacher to his children but also a good example. Early in his journey to create Freedom Mortgage, Stan met Reverend D. Alvin Stewart, who was the head of a men's homeless shelter in Camden, New Jersey, that was having financial and other problems. Stan made a donation to the shelter and started to collect a can of food from each of his mortgage customers to help the shelter. While his own contribution was small, Stan's example led to other, larger donations and expressions of support, ncluding establishing Freedom Cares, which engaged Freedom Mortgage employees to support communities through several annual campaigns. As time as gone on, giving back remains a top priority for Stan as he lives out all seven of his principles.

CHAPTER 7

JOBS AND INFLATION

TIMELINE

1996 Freedom Mortgage reaches one hundred employees
and $10 million in revenue

1999 Mortgage servicing portfolio reaches $83 million

2000 Launches Secondary Marketing and Wholesale channels for buying loans

2001 FOMC drops interest rates down to 1 percent

A big turning point in Stan's professional life in terms of understanding and managing economic cycles came in the early 1990s when he got to hear former Federal Reserve Board chairman Paul Volcker speak. General Electric (GE) had become the largest loan servicer in the United States in that decade of slow economic growth, a little-known fact that provides context to the development of housing finance since the 2000s. Stan's growing mortgage firm was a customer of GE.

"There was an event sponsored by GE and my friend Abe Koch, who was head of the GE secondary markets desk at that time," Stan recalled in a 2019 interview. "We went to this dinner and Bear Stearns's Chief Economist Larry Kudlow was on a panel before the dinner. It was a great event with a lot of people from the finance industry with some interesting conversations."

Volcker was the keynote speaker, Stan recalled: "After leaving the Fed, chairman Volcker had started an effort focused on fostering public service. He was on the speaking circuit taking a victory lap for his handling of inflation. Not all Americans in those days were fans of Volcker. He cost a lot of people their livelihoods in the housing market, for example, because of the terrible economic and labor market fallout from closing down hundreds of S&Ls, mortgage companies, and home builders. And that is just the short list."

In the salons of Washington and Wall Street during the 1980s and 1990s, Chairman Volcker used to joke about how during the Fed's battle with inflation, he received a large piece of wood from an aggrieved citizen who compared the Fed's high interest rate policies to the crucifixion of Jesus Christ. His decisive action on inflation became a model for public servants for decades to come, but sadly, America's willingness to sacrifice to defend consumers from inflation has waned since that time.

"Volcker's comments illuminated my understanding of the economy and how it became a predictor for what happens next and thus played a central role in our business at Freedom Mortgage," said Stan in a thoughtful moment. "Volcker said that the mandate at the Fed may appear to be complicated, but in reality, it is very simple. We have a dual mandate to make sure that inflation does not get out of control and unemployment does not get too high. Our job is to keep unemployment low and inflation low, and we use financial tools to manage those two mandates. I'll always remember his simple, no-nonsense description of economic mechanics."

During the early years of building Freedom Mortgage, Chairman Volcker's clear and straightforward comments were a breath of fresh air for Stan. Until that time, he and other business owners were lost when it came to understanding the economy and how interest rates affected the mortgage business. Things were especially muddled after the S&L crisis and Volcker's use of high interest rates to tame inflation. After hearing Volcker's frank discussion of the Fed's mandate, Stan managed his business tactically and thought about long-term strategy, that is to say, looking around corners, based upon the two basic rules of inflation and jobs.

Chairman Volcker left the Federal Reserve Board in 1989, and Alan Greenspan became the chairman and began the slow reduction of interest rates toward zero. At the very end of the 1990s, the Federal Reserve allowed US interest rates to decline a bit, but by the last month of the twentieth century, short-term interest rates again started to climb and bond investors retreated. The Federal Reserve under Chairman Greenspan signaled concern about rising inflation, suggesting a series of interest rate hikes lay ahead. These were difficult times for independent mortgage bankers like Stan, who were trying to build a business but always had to be ready to trim expenses when the economy overheated and the Fed tapped the brakes.

This tightening of rates by the FOMC hurt mortgage lending volumes as 2000 began and eventually pushed the country into a prolonged economic recession. Yet, even with the higher interest rates and also the slowdown in the economy that continued into 2001, people at that time still expected home prices to appreciate. And important to the next part of our story, there were many parts of the country that still had not recovered from the resolution of the S&L bust of a decade before. In these communities around the United States, there was enormous pent-up demand and need for housing.

At this time, Stan and many other lenders pondered why people in the late 1990s expected higher home prices. There were several answers. First, there was still considerable wage and consumer price inflation, even though chairman Volcker had supposedly "vanquished" inflation. There was also a profound lack of supply of new homes. Cleaning up the S&Ls in the early 1990s also put a damper on home building and thus home lending for years thereafter, but there were other trends and currents that were boosting economic growth.

Eventually, a resurgent economy would push residential home prices higher—part of the American love affair with owning, selling, and financing residential homes. Stan grew up in this difficult environment and was therefore ready to takefull advantage of the opportunities when interest rates fell and lending volumes rose. Mortgage lenders did $1.3 trillion in new loan production in 1993, a huge year for the industry in those days.

The momentum was not maintained in subsequent years, however, when interest rates touched 10 percent and lending volumes fell into the doldrums. In addition, the economic consequences of Paul Volcker's get-tough policy on inflation, using double-digit interest rates to kill expectations for future prices, caused a lot of collateral damage in the world of housing finance, construction, and property development.

Another factor besides consumer demand that helped push housing prices higher was the explosion of new innovations in the world of mortgage finance. The technological advances that began in the late 1980s were really accelerating by this time, with all sorts of new gadgets that helped facilitate the credit underwriting and business processes. Suddenly office workers had all sorts of new electronic devices. But they were part of a larger revolution in consumer finance that stretched back half a century to the years after World War II, when a few large banks controlled most of finance. A Harvard Business School white paper described the evolution of unsecured consumer finance this way:

Banks first began offering credit cards tied to revolving credit accounts in the mid-1950s. Initially, these were marketed to small retailers as a way to allow them to compete with larger stores that offered in-house credit. A decade later, in 1967, an estimated 1,500 banks were offering credit cards, and 11–13 million of these were in active use. Two major bank card networks emerged—BankAmericard (later VISA) in 1965 and Interbank (later MasterCard) in 1967. By 1969 these two networks included 44 million cardholders. Including retail and travel and leisure cards, the total number of cards in use at the time was estimated at 400 million, or roughly three for every adult. Over time, credit card transactions would come to rival the traditional check-based payment system. Electronic transactions (credit cards, debit cards, electronic funds transfers) surpassed check transactions in number in 2003.[17]

During these years, Stan and his colleagues in the mortgage banking business witnessed the miraculous birth of the cell phone and other tools. There was a feeling of excitement, not just in the investment world but among the population generally as well. By the mid-1990s, for example, Fannie Mae and Freddie Mac could access credit scores electronically, an amazing step forward at the time.

Whereas the 1980s and early 1990s had been a tough time for many businesses and families, the late 1990s were a time of rising optimism and expanding horizons albeit tempered with a number

---

17   Andrea Ryan, Gunnar Trumbull, and Peter Tufano, "A Brief Postwar History of US Consumer Finance," Harvard Business School, Working Paper 11-058, 2010, https://www.hbs.edu/faculty/publication%20files/11-058.pdf.

of troubling financial market events. There was an anticipation of economic growth, but there was also a growing awareness that some people were being left behind as prosperity returned.

In the late 1990s, though, consumer credit was not broadly available. People who had equity in their homes still could not get loans to refinance their mortgages. There were people who wanted to buy homes who could not get access to credit, either from a bank or from a mortgage firm. Another factor to accessing mortgage credit in that period besides the level of interest rates was that a lot of people came out of the 1980s and 1990s with bruised credit scores. When it comes to working with consumers with weak credit histories, the mortgage finance system was still relatively dysfunctional three decades ago compared to today. Yet, there was a growing volume of new home building going on in the late 1990s and a feeling that the economy was alive after years of constraint. There was also a huge amount of accumulated demand for new home construction around the country.

The rising optimism of the late 1990s made lenders like Stan feel good about extending credit and lending on high loan-to-values or LTVs, which measure how much cash a homeowner puts down to buy a home. There were a lot of home improvement loans being made in the late 1990s and a shortage of inventory of homes, much as we see today. The process of resolving hundreds of failed S&Ls also meant the liquidation of many developers and home builders.

Stan learned during this period that the ebb and flow of markets and interest rates could be dangerous for even the best business operators. In 1996, for example, US accounting rules were changed to allow lenders to recognize all of the profits from the sale of a loan up front, before the cash arrived every month over the life of the loan. This meant that you reported a profit but had not actually received the cash. You sold the mortgage note into the bond market and retained the servicing rights, booking the discounted present value up front.

There were a number of nonbanks that took advantage of this change and went from zero to hero overnight. They raised a lot of money or in some cases went public based upon wildly optimistic financials and "earnings" assumptions. These companies were not so different from fintech lenders and the proliferation of fringe consumer lenders that came two decades later in the early 2020s. When the liquidity crisis hit, however, many of these companies folded.

Gain-on-sale accounting and stated "earnings" were not the same thing as cold, hard cash, Stan recalled in a 2020 interview. Many of these consumer lenders and also some nonbank mortgage companies went out of business by the time the 2000s began. While some lenders in that period experienced problems, Stan's conservative view of the market was proven correct. The assets that were created by lenders such as Freedom Mortgage in the late 1990s and early 2000s were "money good," meaning that the home prices were stable and supported the value of the loans. By no coincidence, Freedom Mortgage reached its first billion in servicing in 2003.

Home prices did appreciate, and the value of the mortgage collateral turned out to be quite solid. The rising inflation of home values covered a lot of sins in terms of the actual credit of the borrower. And overall, defaulted loans in that period of the late 1990s were extremely low, and the value of homes kept postdefault loan recovery rates strong. Stan talks about that period:

"At Freedom Mortgage, we held second lien mortgages on our books with 15 percent annual coupon rates that paid for ten years. In retrospect, my only question was why couldn't I keep more of those loans! We funded those loans with cash capital because there was no liquidity for them, but they turned out to be money good assets and a great investment for the company."

When you look at the high rate of attrition among subprime lenders in the finance company sector during the late 1990s and then after the subprime crisis in 2008, the common thread in the story is that these firms came in to provide financing to borrowers who couldn't get a mortgage from a commercial bank and could not even work with a nonbank mortgage lender. These were borrowers on the bleeding edge of subprime lending, with the commensurate risks. Stan Middleman, throughout his entire career, has been careful not to stand on the bleeding edge of finance and also observed its ebb and flow as a key market indicator.

The nonbank lenders filled the gap for people who had lesser credit and higher LTVs in their home mortgages. Firms such as Citibank, Countrywide, Wells Fargo (which merged with Norwest in 1998), and others provided the financing. While the subprime lending market started in the 1990s, it didn't begin to take shape until the early 2000s, accounting for 6 percent of all residential mortgage originations, the San Francisco Fed reported. By 2006, subprime originations comprised 25 percent of all mortgage loan originations that year and 14 percent of the overall mortgage market.[18] And yet, for many Americans, getting a mortgage was still not even seen as an option.

"Many consumers couldn't get new first lien loans, consolidate their bills, or get second mortgages, so the next stop was personal loans," Stan recalls of that era. "These personal loans, however, effectively became mezzanine financing on the homes, almost like a third mortgage in some cases. Watching the movement of interest rates and home prices

---

18   Federal Reserve Bank of San Francisco Annual Report, "The Subprime Mortgage Market," 2007, www.frbsf.org/wp-content/uploads/2007annualreport.pdf.

gave you a big hint that liquidity problems would eventually cause difficulties in the fringe products around the mortgage sector."

The Art of Operations

When Freedom Mortgage got its first agency approval from Freddie Mac three decades ago, it was a huge achievement for the company and Stan. Being a third-party originator or "TPO" means that you are a licensed originator of mortgage loans who does not have a Seller agreement or Seller/Servicer number with Fannie Mae or Freddie Mac. Freedom Mortgage becaome a full-fledged member of the mortgage club, dealing directly with the government-sponsored entities (GSEs) as a counterparty.

The approvals from first Freddie Mac and then Fannie Mae triggered licensing approvals by the states. As Freedom Mortgage gained the approval of more and more states, they were better able to generate volumes and manage the risks in terms of economic and credit cycles at the state and even local levels. The dream of creating a national mortgage business was starting to come within reach.

"Sometimes a region of the country was really hot, other times it might be in a recession," recalls Stan of the period of geographic expansion. "But gaining access to these new markets was only the beginning of the journey. We had to sell ourselves to the banks and to investors as well. This meant early on making the decision to reinvest our profits back into the business in order to build our financial capital and also our team."

As noted earlier, the late 1990s saw a lot of changes in the world of mortgage finance and banking more generally. The composition of mortgage companies changed as technology began to support many clerical functions. They could print, fax, and eventually scan documents. The miles of aisles and desks and printers and copies and fax machines began to change. People prepared their own letters on their own printers. The operating efficiency and *leverage* in the workplace really began to grow. And in that era, mortgage banks began to think and talk about how many performing loans a person could service every month.

"The rise of General Electric saw the first $100 billion servicer of loans in the financial services industry," recalls Stan. "In 1990, keep in mind, the entire US mortgage industry did less than $500 billion in mortgage originations in a year, so a $100 billion servicing book was pretty big."

After the death and restructuring of the S&Ls, a billion dollars was still considered a lot of money in the early 2000s. GE had substantial market share, especially for a nonbank, but the big commercial banks still owned the back office of servicing and collateral finance related to mortgage lending. Even in those days, the independent mortgage bankers made the loans, but the commercial banks acquired and financed loans, often holding them as investments to maturity.

What GE did have was a lot of cash flow generated by a variety of big-ticket products. At the start of the 2000s, GE owned General Electric Capital Corporation (GE Capital), Employers Reinsurance Corporation, and the investment banking firm Kidder, Peabody. Imagine GE Capital at $100 billion in assets under management as a big deal in the mid-1990s. Today we talk about J.P. Morgan Chase or Wells Fargo at more than $1 trillion in total mortgage servicing, and banks still account for more than half of the mortgage servicing pie.

Countrywide Financial reached $1.5 trillion in servicing before it was acquired by Bank of America. Freedom Mortgage at the end of 2023 was proud to service the mortgages of two million homeowners, representing over $460 billion in loans. Over the past twenty-five years, the industry has been enormously consolidated, largely by commercial banks as well as by nonbank lenders and real estate investment trusts (REITs). Names that were dominant two decades ago like Countrywide and GE have long since disappeared from the world of mortgage lending. And today, the newer, more effective nonbanks like Rocket Mortgage, Mr. Cooper, and Freedom Mortgage take a larger share of the servicing market.

In order to drive the consolidation of the mortgage servicing sector, Stan notes, there was a steady and continuous effort to achieve more productivity. GE had hundreds of thousands of square feet of offices and thousands of employees. A lot of the work had to be done manually, even with the rise of technology and the creation of new tools. Today, nonbanks like Freedom Mortgage, Quicken, and Penny Mac are able to underwrite and service many more loans than GE did a quarter of a century ago and with far fewer people. Stan recalls what it was like to process loans in that period:

"In the 1990s, everything still had to be done by hand. Calculations had to be made and verified multiple times. Envelopes had to be sent. We became more efficient by building massive operations for printing and folding paper documents. As little as five years ago, Wells Fargo had the most efficient print shop in our industry. It's just crazy when you think about how we did business twenty-five years ago and how the mortgage industry moves data and documents in 2024. These were big companies that were well organized and managed, but by today's standards had enormous inefficiencies built into their systems. Companies performed efficiency studies and analyzed the position of people on the floor, but it was only with the empowerment of the computer that we began to see real change in terms of the operations of mortgage companies."

By the time the mortgage industry reached the 2000s, mortgage banks were able to do much more than ever before by leveraging technology and improving people, from the chief executives right down to the team on the servicing floor or the call center. Everyone needed to learn about new technology and how to apply these new methods of thinking and working to service customers and partners in the correspondent channel. By the 2000s, Freedom Mortgage was working with dozens of other nonbank mortgage companies as correspondents, which means that they were originating and selling loans using Freedom Mortgage's document template and Freedom Mortgage's underwriting guidelines.

Another big change that occurred in the 2000s because of new technology was the need to interact face-to-face with consumers really changed. The world of networking and nexus marketing that had served Stan a decade before while selling annuities was changing rapidly. He tells the fascinating tale of how Freedom Mortgage managed sales calls:

> "In the very early days operating a call center, we had our loan officers or 'LOs' call to make appointments on Sunday nights, Saturday mornings, and Friday afternoons. They scheduled all of their appointments for the following week. The idea was to get to two or three or if they were lucky four customers in a day. We'd try to come home with a sale or two every day. Our salesforce was very good at qualifying leads and closing sales. We tried to constantly stay ahead of the curve in terms of sales techniques and operations. Not everybody organized their calling effort or helped the staff organize calls geographically."

Stan would give the sales staff rolls of quarters so that they could call from a pay phone to check in after each call and update their schedule. Freedom Mortgage had a central dispatcher who would send the salespeople to the next appointment. This was revolutionary two decades ago. They'd get into the car with their map and figure out how to get to the next call. Stan's team had maps on the walls of the office with pins for each salesperson. They needed to get a real, "wet" signature on the loan application before the process could begin. But the mortgage industry was about to surge forward into the roaring 2000s.

Living in Tomorrow

In 2000, Freedom Mortgage was a decade old and had reached the point where the team's execution was fairly reliable. Stan could count on the people and organization that he had groomed to execute the plan and run the business day to day. The details and focus required to run a mortgage banking firm are extremely demanding. Industry observer Rob Chrisman put it well in his daily commentary in August 2020 during the darkest part of the COVID-19 pandemic:

> No one owns a crystal ball. It seems that the best LOs and CEOs keep up on the news and trends but focus on helping borrowers one at a time, regardless of predictions. If anyone predicted six months ago that a) the world would still find itself grappling with a pandemic, and b) urban home values would be suffering while suburban and country house prices would be escalating, I missed it.[19]

---

19 Rob Chrisman, "Ops, TPO Sales Jobs; Forbearance, Correspondent, Title, Broker Products; Lots of Training & Virtual Events," August 31, 2020, https://www.robchrisman.com/aug-31-ops-tpo-sales-jobs-forbearance-correspondent-title-broker-products-lots-of-training-virtual-events/.

When you have a team that can run the business day to day, that's when you as the owner of a mortgage firm must evolve into a full-time strategist and top-level risk manager, Stan believes. The strategy role begins with top-level concerns, the direction of the economy, and interest rates, for example. Based on those inputs, you can then start to think about the business and its resources and needs, thinking ahead two and three years into the future.

Strategists rely on a toolbox that contains a whole bevy of things that we've previously discussed, tools that let you manage today and prepare for tomorrow. This includes creating a team with expertise and management skills for complex tasks, tactics, and completing tasks efficiently, and who are interested in becoming a leader. Building people who can execute the tasks required is crucial, Stan maintains. Developing tacticians and managers in different disciplines is vital to achieve implementation, to ensure the accurate execution of the plan that comes down from the strategist.

All of those things really need to be in place for someone to do a great job of developing strategy, Stan continues. In the mortgage business where every loan is different, you must manage each relationship as a precious asset, whether that relationship is with a consumer or an investor. Like good ideas, strategies without qualitative implementation and professional execution are often just a waste of space and time, especially in an industry like consumer lending where imperfection is not tolerated and apparently innocent errors can carry big costs.

Poor execution can readily lead to failure. But having the confidence as the strategist that the organization will execute the chosen plan is a fundamental bedrock of being able to do your job as a leader in a fairly mature and large organization. You can only build a strategy for tomorrow, Stan argues, if the business is being managed today.

This leads us to the seventh and perhaps most important of Stan's principles, namely, 'Living in Tomorrow.'

"Once you've reached that point, you really start to zero in on building true, repeatable, sustainable success and growth, because now you're able to devote almost all of your energy to the place where success lives, and that's tomorrow," says Stan. He continues:

> We've said that today really is a given. Everything that happens today, you can't really change or shape or alter, because all the work and thought has gone into it far before today. But if you're spending today trying to plan what you're going to do today, then you are truly likely to fail. Success is born in preparation and in thought and opportunity evaluation of the future. Your recognition of the environment and sensitivity and awareness to all those things around you, and the way those things would expect to become drives your perspective. And that's called living in tomorrow.

People who are most successful and have built the most sustainable businesses all spend most of their time living in tomorrow, Stan believes. There're lots of things that get in the way of that, lots of examples of companies that stopped growing, that tried to sustain success based on their *past success*. Stan feels strongly that you can live in tomorrow and be wrong-minded:

"When we talk about being a person that lives in tomorrow, today is not the essence of tomorrow. That's a big step and a big challenge to wrap your brain around. But the simple truth is that when you've had some success and things have gone well, your propensity is to try and build tomorrow by creating or sustaining more of the same."

Stan holds up Sears as a great example of a business managed for today or even yesterday that has since disappeared. The number of successful public companies over the past half century is likewise a small subset of the total. But there're numerous examples of other companies that get so caught up in what they're doing that today becomes tomorrow because it's sucking up all of their energy.

Another example that comes to mind is Eastman Kodak. Mortgage firms such as Countrywide and GE are also examples of firms that took their eye off the ball in terms of thinking about future risk. These once great firms were not leading their management teams to the job of expanding from today, from the implementation of the plan to the creation of a strategy for tomorrow. Thus, Countrywide became the buyer of other people's problems in the 1990s, replacing Citibank in the 1980s.

When you're a small business, all the responsibility for managing the company and having a strategy can and usually does rest in an individual, and that's a challenging environment. Most businesses fail because of the loss of an important individual, what we call "key man" risk. That's precisely where Stan's journey began in Philadelphia in the 1980s. The agility of being a one-man band allows you to move smoothly from one skill to the next, exercising one piece of your responsibility to the next. Generally, you don't do it as successfully, as reliably, as sustainably as does an organization.

"Yet you have greater agility the smaller your group, the ability to move more smoothly from strategy to implementation to task to execution to tactic of execution," Stan reflects. "The smaller the organization, the more agility, but the less the operating leverage. The larger the organization, the less agility, but the more leverage is possible of people and systems. The more successful the organization, the more likely the strategist gets sucked into implementation and execution. That's where companies, organizations, individuals impair their success and impede and even imperil their future."

The business only becomes a living, breathing organism once it reaches a certain size and mass, Stan observes after several decades in business. To focus on tomorrow is a critical element for anybody who's running a midsize or large organization. The need to keep the mind clear, and constantly focus on tomorrow so that the company can be growing, living, breathing, is a challenge. By not making tomorrow a function necessarily of today, you challenge your assumptions and plans and manage risk as part of that process. Stan believes that it's very difficult to separate those ideas about strategy because tomorrow's environment, in all likelihood, won't be today's environment. Tomorrow's opportunities, in all likelihood, will not be today's opportunities.

"The lesson learned in cycles is that opportunities come around multiple times," says Stan thoughtfully. "Economic periods kind of go in a cyclical fashion, with interest rates and employment rising and falling, which impacts credit quality and business volumes. It's a merry-go-round of risk, meaning they come back around over and over, but perhaps in different order or scale. If you're dealing with yesterday's part of the cycle by trying to do more of it tomorrow, the cycle moves and changes, and the environment changes. What is appropriate today may not be apropos tomorrow, leaving you at risk."

Stan feels that where companies, financial organizations, and, to a great extent, funds and fund managers really fall by the wayside is by saying, "This is what I'm doing. It works. I want to do more of it."

Stan's point is that focusing on today is why you see so many industry classes and so many businesses and so many industries evolve into a monoculture of closely comparable business models. In the same way that consultants routinely overvalue mortgage servicing assets to please the vanity of Wall Street, the typical business manager clusters and crowds around the latest business model, thinking this is a safe bet. But, in fact, it is the worst possible strategy.

"We call these copycat industries where somebody does something that works and then you copy what they do," relates Stan, who sees such behavior as self-defeating. "Well, if you didn't come up with the original thought, you may not know why you're being successful. If you didn't implement the strategy based on environmental sensitivity and awareness beyond 'It worked for somebody else,' how can you intellectually believe you'll be prepared when the environment changes? That leaves you strictly as having limited success for as long as the current environment lasts."

To merely exploit current success may be enough for some people, but it doesn't create a sustainable level of achievement, Stan argues—a red flag either for an individual or for a business. Living in today doesn't create the time and the financial freedom to make good plans and good decisions to implement those plans. By managing the business carefully and with sensitivity to risks and rewards, you enable agility of thought and make the organization responsive. That's why our earlier discussion around change was so important, because a great organization is constantly evolving and maturing. Stan feels that we should live in the deepest fear of not growing and changing, especially in the world of consumer finance.

"When we talked about fearlessness earlier, we talked about it in relation to embracing change, not being afraid to change," Stan opines. "Fear is a great catalyst to planning. Fear that your current success will abate, or the tide will go out, or ebb, is a tremendous motivator to strategic thinking and planning for tomorrow. Fear forces you to look and build a list of the opportunities and the dangers facing your business."

While the world of mortgage lending is basically a fixed margin business that rewards efficient manufacturers of loans and servicing assets, the focus on optimizing operations is the enemy of living in tomorrow. Where is the world, the market, your environment moving next year or in the next decade? Where is it going, and how does that impact you? What is going to happen next?

For Stan Middleman, asking those questions every day embodies living in tomorrow and enables you to start to see around corners. You have to be, if you're the strategist, firmly planted in tomorrow and question the viability of today's business, successful or not. What can I do to create opportunity and avoid risk? This is the biggest question Stan asks himself each and every day.

In living for tomorrow, Stan thinks it's important to write down, to visualize, to completely understand each of the next phases of the cycle, and to try to project time frames that those next phases will occur, the length that they will last, and the way you can respond to them, whether or not you have time to tactically, and on a task-oriented basis, respond to those issues that are before you. That is incredibly difficult and stressful and a straining type of thought. Again, it's important to critically look at your business, the business that you're operating in today, and ask, "What makes the most sense? What are the elements that I need?"

Well, if you're going to need to have capital, you may need to have four or five years' runway to raise that capital before you're ready to fully deploy it in the fashion that you hope to. You may have to raise the capital and create a short-term plan and a longer-term plan for its use, because when you're ready to deploy it and you need it, it may not be available. It is easy to raise money when you don't need it, as the old axiom goes.

The cycles also make the raising of debt and equity more challenging at different points in time. Judging how and when to access the financial markets for new capital is one of the most difficult decisions facing any manager. As Freedom Mortgage entered the 2000s, Stan and his team needed to keep increasing their knowledge and sophistication as a business. Past success was nice but not sufficient. To keep up with the strong housing growth that the mortgage industry would see in the first decade of the twenty-first century, Freedom Mortgage needed to run faster.

CHAPTER 8

THE MERRY-GO-ROUND OF RISK

TIMELINE

2001	Dot-com bubble bursts; FOMC cuts short-term interest rates eleven times
2002	Freedom Mortgage acquires first mortgage servicing portfolio
2003	Head count reaches five hundred employees, and servicing portfolio tops $1 billion
2006	Freedom Mortgage acquires Irwin Mortgage, adds 1,500 people, $12 billion in revenue
2004	Mortgage originations peak
2005	Loan quality deteriorates; Freedom Mortgage shuts down California offices

Until the end of the 1990s, there was very little new home construction in the United States and thus a lot of unmet demand from consumers *and* investors. It was a situation not entirely dissimilar to what we see in the 2020s in terms of a lack of construction of new affordable housing. This shortage of inventory would soon explode into the lending and building boom of the early 2000s that led directly to the 2008 financial crisis. Stan described the merry-go-round of risk:

The more things change in housing, the more things stay the same or at least repeat in cycles. In the spring of 2020, the market was already heating up. We saw the return of streamlined nonqualified mortgage refinance products that require no verifications or documentation from the borrower. Just as risk is a merry-go-round, so too is the mortgage business, home construction and all other aspects of housing finance move in cycles, but with sometimes significant changes in each period.

At the end of the 1990s, the dot-com bubble started to blow up in the equity markets, and the markets saw a liquidity crisis caused by Russia's default in the fall of 1998. Yet, the Fed would continue raising interest rates from the fall of 1998 right through to the end of 2000, causing a recession. Yet, rising interest rates were a boon to Stan and Freedom Mortgage. At the end of 1999, Freedom Mortgage sold a substantial block of mortgage servicing that took the company out of debt and increased the firm's net worth. Stan sold MSRs created earlier in the decade for 7× annual cash flow. He had originally booked these MSRs at 1× cash flow when the loans were sold. As interest rates fell and prices for seasoned MSRs declined, Stan again began to accumulate servicing assets as new loans were sold.

Consumer lenders such as Citibank saw default rates rise substantially. Despite the two-point increase in rates from 1998 through 2000, however, there was a new flow of credit coming into the mortgage market from a variety of unconventional lenders. This is what Stan refers to as "fringe finance," which would explode into a surge of new loan types.

"While banks generally were not lending in the late 1990s," recalls Stan in a 2019 interview, "nonbanks were in the market in a veritable coral reef of traditional consumer lenders. Hard money lenders, personal loan lenders such as HFC, Beneficial, even banks such as Manufacturers Hanover, were making second mortgage loans and getting into other 'fringe' products. First mortgages were still really hard to get a decade after the S&L crisis. Then we started to see debt consolidation loans and other forms of innovation. This allowed people to use the equity in their home to pay off high-rate credit cards and consumer loans."

In 2000, Citibank acquired Associates, which was the former consumer finance arm of Ford Motor Co. The tactics used by some of these traditional consumer lenders were grafted onto the mortgage industry during the subprime lending boom of 2000 through 2004, with profoundly bad results a decade later. Associates eventually was pilloried on *60 Minutes* for extending excessive number of loans to a homeowner, charging multiple fees until the borrower lost their home to foreclosure.

In the early 2000s, however, the subprime mortgage party was in full swing, and nobody was going to stop it. There was simply too much pent-up consumer demand after more than a decade of austerity and slow housing credit markets. The nature of this overheated market was illustrated by the fact that more than one-third of all loans originated during the 2004–2007 period came from mortgage brokers.[20] Demand for new homes, for building new developments, for lending on these assets and issuing new mortgage securities was enormous. The entire housing food chain, combined with demographics, would cause lending volumes to rise threefold in a matter of months.

Debt was another factor. A lot of people had run up personal debts in the 1990s, when the value of homes had fallen. A huge opportunity was created in the 2000s for consumer lenders once value came

---

20   John Bancroft, "Wholesale-Broker Channel Gains Ground in 2Q23 Rally," Inside Mortgage Finance, August 25, 2023, https://www.insidemortgagefinance.com/articles/228688-wholesale-broker-channel-gains-ground-in-2q23-rally?v=preview.

back to those same homes. Driven by a lack of inventory, the value of homes started to climb near the end of the decade. That fact fueled the surge in mortgage activity in the early 2000s. Stan Middleman saw a huge jump in home price appreciation in this period, making him even more confident that the loans and servicing assets he was accumulating would be money good investments to support the company when the economy slowed.

As the economy did slow in 2001, interest rates fell dramatically, mortgage lending exploded, and Stan and his team were ready. At the end of 2000, the Fed funds rate was at 6.5 percent, but by the end of 2001, Alan Greenspan had pushed short-term interest rates down below 2 percent until the federal funds rate reached just 1 percent. Unemployment rose, rates fell, and housing led the United States out of the brief 2001 recession.

"The liquidity crisis that occurred at the end of the 1990s caused a number of nonbank lenders, finance companies mostly, to fail," Stan says of that difficult period in the economy. "A lot of nonbanks did what were called 125 LTV loans. This was where the loan—usually a first mortgage—had a loan amount equal to 125 percent of the initial property value. When the liquidity dried up in 1998 and 1999, these nonbanks that were focused on such fringe subprime products failed in large numbers. These firms failed because of the business model."

The lesson that Stan took from Chairman Volcker in the early 1990s helped him to navigate the market volatility of the early 2000s and anticipate the 2008 financial crisis by several years. That period, decades earlier—from the October 1987 stock market selloff through into 1989 when Paul Volcker left the Fed—saw a major asset correction in mortgages and other assets, with all of the attendant collateral damages that such market contagion entails. People lost jobs, companies went bust, and the entire economy was in a stagnant phase for years.

As the 1990s began, mortgage interest rates were still in double digits, as was inflation. However, that turmoil in credit markets created a lot of opportunities for entrepreneurs like Stan Middleman and other independent mortgage banks that started in those difficult years. Many of the survivors of that period would become the dominant players in the mortgage industry after 2008.

"In financial history, liquidity problems seem to develop around the years ending with the number eight," Stan half jokes but also in a serious vein. "First, we saw October 1987 and the S&L crisis, then a decade later the Russian debt default in 1998, then the 2008 subprime financial crisis, and then the liquidity crises in the waning weeks of 2018, then the outbreak of COVID in 2020. In each case, interest rates fell dramatically, creating a boom in housing."

If you watch the basic ebb and flow of liquidity and how it reacts to changes in employment, interest rates, and, increasingly, headlines and crises, Stan argues, then you start to discern a pattern. And, as Stan loves to say, no genius is required to observe this phenomenon at work in the markets. You simply need to be aware and sensitive to what's happening around you, to your customers, partners, and the other businesses you touch.

If you track the trends for interest rates and employment, the results have been almost perfectly aligned with the outcomes in terms of the economy. In Stan's mind, if a manager follows the Fed's dual mandate in even a cursory sort of way, the economy and also the mortgage market are not so difficult to understand. Yet, very few people think about the economy that way or about what it will look like in the next year or five years out. Some people even express surprise at the Fed's decisions on interest rates, but to Stan, as the manager of a business working in housing finance, the key thing has been and remains to follow the Fed in terms of economic trends.

When unemployment rises, that will impact the Fed's policy reaction and also important things like the next election, which impacts public policy. The dramatically higher level of unemployment will drive interest rates down and keep them down for an extended period. Yet, as Stan likes to say, "then things change," and the change in Fed policy after COVID-19 is perhaps the most dramatic shift in the history of the US central bank.

"The recession after 2008 and subsequent recovery drove up the value of housing assets because of latent demand," Stan believes. He compares the 2010s with the 1990s in terms of the slow recovery of demand for housing and new construction. "And that demand, combined with lower interest rates, eventually led us out of the recession and even kept the period of actual contraction very short. To me, it was kind of a done deal, but to many people the ebb and flow of the economy remains a mystery."

Following trends in unemployment told Stan and his team how to react in terms of managing the business. In the early days after Freedom Mortgage's founding, the United States was still coming off a recession. Housing did not initially really lead the way out in terms of recovery of consumer activity or jobs. Stan likes to remind people that there had not yet been a *value recovery* in terms of home prices until late in the decade.

When Stan and other mortgage bankers use terms like "money good" and "valuation recovery," they generally refer to the current market value of the collateral—the house—which secures the mortgage note. There are typically two pieces to a mortgage loan: the *mort-gage* (Latin for "unto death"), which attaches a lien onto a piece of property, and the mortgage note, which evidences the borrowing and is often financed in the debt markets.

The liquidity crisis in the late 1990s stemmed from a crisis among fringe finance products, Stan maintains, not from mainstream residential mortgages. And, as Stan argues passionately, a similar opportunity lies ahead in the mortgage market in the 2020s as America learns to live with higher interest rates and home prices that resulted from the response to COVID-19 and other factors. Among other things, this "new normal" will make servicing assets even more valuable.

Mortgage bankers need to appreciate that a correction in the price of fringe financial products and assets is not the same thing as a major correction in home prices, Stan argues, like we saw in the late 1980s and after 2008. At the end of 1998, there was a big price correction in new, "unconventional" financial products, but the stage was set almost immediately for a major rebound. A surge in housing activity occurred in the early 2000s as interest rates fell and pent-up demand for housing pulled prices higher.

"The Russian liquidity crisis in 1998 was also the death knell for some types of subprime lending in the US for several years," Stan describes the market at that time. "Second mortgages and even high loan-to-value (LTV) first lien mortgages had become popular during the previous decade of tight bank credit in the 1990s. These were all nontraditional or 'fringe' products originated outside of the bank and agency market. But the demand was there because most consumers could not get a loan from a bank."

A lot of companies that were marketing fringe financial products in 1998 saw the market evaporate, but the mainstream assets in the mortgage sector—that is, homes—were still money good and continued to grow in value for the next decade until the 2008 market break. As we'll discuss, the mortgage market actually began to retreat several years before the great financial crisis—yet another example of Stan's credo of seeing around corners. But you must look in order to see.

Almost immediately after the 1998 debt crisis passed and the 2000s began, the mortgage industry surged. By 2003, interest rates had fallen to the lowest levels in a generation, setting off a boom in terms of mortgage originations. The sharp decline in interest rates engineered by Fed chairman Alan Greenspan, however, was a nasty surprise for bond investors. The thirty-year mortgage rate fell below 5.25 percent—at that time the record low—which put virtually all outstanding mortgages in the United States in the money for refinance. When we say a mortgage is "in the money," that means that current market interest rates are below the rate a consumer is paying. If you think of a mortgage loan like a bond, when interest rates fall, the value of older, higher coupon mortgages goes up. That market premium can be converted into a lower interest rate for the borrower.

> When the Fed dropped interest rates early in the 2000s, mortgage bond prices soared, handing principal losses to investors around the globe. Every time a homeowner refinanced, the Bank of Japan and other central banks that purchase Ginnie Mae mortgage bonds lost money. Many home mortgages were prepaid that summer, causing joy to lenders and realtors and misery for bond investors around the world.

Pent-up demand for housing going back to the mid-1980s drove a housing boom in the 2000s, a manic explosion of demand for shelter—and demand for bonds on Wall Street—that eventually resulted in a massive asset correction. The great financial crisis that came a few years later was so enormous in impact because it was a major correction of the entire housing market. At the time, half the market was composed of what the industry calls "private-label" mortgages with no government backing. When the music stopped at the end of 2007, the stage was set for disaster—and lower interest rates for a decade to come.

The decade following the 2008 financial crisis was very similar to the late 1980s and 1990s, in that there was a big correction followed by a long period of recovery and, at first, little growth in mortgage lending, new construction, or home prices. Housing did not lead the United States out of the 2008 recession; rather, fringe assets such as personal loans, student loans, and auto loans grew strongly. Indeed, the total amount of credit available to housing from banks and the bond markets actually fell and then stagnated for most of the 2010s. Mortgage credit only really began to grow again at the end of the decade. By 2018, when loan profitability reached all-time lows, mortgage volumes finally started to grow and drove home prices higher.

"Using the rule of 'the eights,' history suggests that 2028 will be the year of the correction—at least until COVID-19 arrived on the scene," Stan observes. "As we've discussed, things change— sometimes without any warning. COVID-19 is the biggest single and most sudden change in my professional life. It brought huge changes in consumer preferences and behavior. As always, we must be very attentive to credit as always as we go forward. But strong home prices give us a lot of confidence that today's home loans will be money good."

Loans and Liquidity

Your ability to raise capital when needed is generally far less than when raising capital prior to needing it. Having a good plan to acquire and deploy liquidity is important to make investors confident in you, Stan has learned over the years, so that they're willing to put capital into the business to support your plan for operations. Whether debt or equity, access to adequate funding is essential for any business, new or old.

Adequate funding provides you and your team the *opportunity* to plan and execute your longer-term strategy. Whether it's your own equity capital or credit lines from the bank or debt raised in the bond market, your ability to access and maintain funding enables you to succeed. In no industry is that more important than in consumer finance, where credit lines from banks fuel and support nonbank lending. Only the largest, oftentimes publicly traded mortgage firms can access the equity and debt markets.

When you consider that Stan Middleman started Freedom Mortgage with basically nothing, his success is all that more remarkable and a true American success story. But it is also a story repeated many times over in what is the largest market in the world for financing homeownership. Housing attracts entrepreneurs, people who are good at sales and operations equally. Mortgage bankers are leaders and managers who love working for and with consumers and who are not afraid to face the brutal vagaries of the financial markets and interest rates that face all nonbank lenders.

In the early 1990s, after Freedom Mortgage won approval to sell conventional loans to Freddie Mac and Fannie Mae, Stan needed to get financing from banks and nonbanks in order to finance loan production and grow. The company's first warehouse line actually came not from a bank but from GE Capital, the financial arm of GE, a fact that might surprise many people today.

When Stan started Freedom Mortgage, GE had a large banking business built around GE Money Bank, including credit card loans and mortgage servicing. Not only was the blue-chip industrial company's finance arm, GE Capital, a major servicer of mortgage loans, but it also provided financing to nonbank lenders as banks do today.

Freedom Mortgage had another line of credit with the Provident of Cincinnati and also had a credit line with the investment bank Dean Witter, but the firm's main financing relationship in those days was with GE Capital. After a decade in business, Stan had carefully accumulated a substantial amount of equity capital. This capital enabled Freedom Mortgage to retain some loans on balance sheet instead of selling immediately into the secondary market.

"We did well in that period of the late 1980s, but we did not acquire assets from failed S&Ls via the Resolution Trust Corp," says Stan of that time. "I stayed in agency product. The only specialty deals we did was through correspondence with banks, which in those days was Citibank. Correspondent lending was our main business in the 1990s."

A "correspondent lender" is a mortgage bank that originates and funds loans in its own name and then sells them to a larger firm such as Freedom Mortgage or J.P. Morgan Chase to eventually go into a mortgage-backed security. In the wholesale channel, on the contrary, as with thrifts and banks such as Citibank in the 1980s and 1990s, a mortgage broker starts the loan process and then passes the "warm" lead to a mortgage bank, which underwrites and closes the loan.

Correspondent lending started as a business in the 1980s when S&Ls were the predominant buyers of third-party loans in the secondary mortgage market. By the mid-1990s, Countrywide rose to the top of the food chain as the buyer of choice in the secondary market, where loans originated by mortgage banks were sold. Countrywide did both broker and correspondent business and quickly became the dominant player in the secondary markets even as Citibank exited the market for a few years in the mid-1990s. Countrywide called themselves "America's wholesale lender" because that is how they built their business.

At that time, independent mortgage banks had something like 40 percent share of the mortgage market, and the banks had the rest. The banks also purchased most of the servicing, if you included Countrywide as a bank, but there were exceptions such as GE Capital. Nonbanks and REITs were not significant owners of mortgage servicing thirty years ago, but then new players such as GE and others entered the scene in a big way in the 2000s. The first five years of the 2000s were a remarkable period of boom for mortgage lending, setting the stage for an equally large asset price correction after the 2008 financial crisis.

"What Do You Want from Me?"

One great example of Stan's discipline of looking around corners and living in tomorrow involves the conventional loan market that exists around GSEs, such as Fannie Mae and Freddie Mac. The GSEs buy loans from lenders and then they guarantee loans and issue mortgage-backed securities (MBSs) to finance them. Today, the conventional loan market served by Fannie and Freddie represents about half of the $13 trillion market for mortgages in the United States. The remainder is the government-insured market of the Federal Housing Administration (FHA), Department of Veterans Affairs (VA), Ginnie Mae, and loans owned by commercial banks in portfolio.

In the early 2000s, the market for home mortgages was largely dominated by the GSEs, but this changed dramatically as privately originated mortgages surged onto the scene. By 2003, many mortgage companies were working flat out to meet the demand from Wall Street and also the GSEs for private mortgage securities, especially those backed by private-label loans with higher yields and no mortgage insurance premiums. In this respect, the demand from the GSEs for private mortgages fueled the housing boom of the early 2000s.

By the mid-2000s, Freedom Mortgage was producing conventional government loans, and also "Alt-A" mortgages. Alt-A lending was a "no-doc" loan as we discussed earlier and was considered riskier than prime loans yet less risky than "subprime." Alt-A loans were used for borrowers such as the self-employed and other borrowers that were outside the traditional prime credit box used by commercial banks and the agencies. If that sounds like the Mortgage Power product of Citibank in the late 1980s and early 1990s, you're correct.

By 2005, the big banks pushed the GSEs out of the way in the secondary market, and private-label mortgages became the largest share of total US mortgage production. GE got into subprime mortgage lending at the height of the craze, selling its loan servicing business to Wells Fargo in 2000, making it the bank the largest servicer of mortgages in the United States, and buying WMC in 2004. WMC originated more than $65 billion in mortgages between 2005 and 2007, many of them private-label. When annual industry production reached nearly $4 trillion, it seemed like the good times would go on forever. But it was not to be. WMC would eventually cost GE billions in losses, fines, and legal settlements because of the poor quality of the firm's loans.[21]

Even as agency and private "Alt-A" loan volumes were still strong in the mid-2000s, Stan and his team consciously started moving Freedom Mortgage's business away from this market and into the relative safety of the government loan market built around the FHA and Ginnie Mae. Why did Stan and his team make this change? Very

---

21   Jonathan Stempel, "GE's WMC Mortgage Unit, Felled by Financial Crisis, Files Chapter 11 Bankruptcy," Reuters.net, April 23, 2019, www.reuters.com/article/us-ge-wmc-bankruptcy/ges-wmc-mortgage-unit-felled-by-financial-crisis-files-chapter-11-bankruptcy-idUSKCN1RZ1OI.

simply, Freedom Mortgage looked ahead, and what they saw made them increasingly uncomfortable.

The first clue that something was amiss came in late 2004, when Freedom Mortgage's credit quality team started to notice a sudden increase in fraudulent loans coming from several offices in California. By this time, sophisticated criminals figured out how to manufacture bogus income verification documents, opening the door to fraudulent loans. After a few weeks of steadily rising incidents of fraudulent loan applications, Freedom Mortgage began to shut down its Alt-A product nationally and literally closed several offices in Southern California by early 2005.

"Loan fraud in the 2004 period was like a virus," Stan remembers. "We saw first one loan a week, then five, then twenty. I literally pulled the plug on several branches in California and had our regional manager layoff the staff. As we saw it, we had no choice. The loan production these offices were doing came from brokers and was mostly Alt-A type loans, so shuttering the business made sense. In the early 2000s, the broker community was the gestation place for loan fraud."

The broker community was essentially outsourced originations, so quality problems were always a concern—even when brokers accounted for half of total originations. The second indicator in terms of risk was coming from the conventional loan market, which at the time was a significant part of Freedom Mortgage's business. "We were becoming concerned that there would be problems with the GSEs, Fannie Mae and Freddie Mac, because we knew from the 1980s that the private mortgage insurers would not pay claims on conventional loans," laments Stan.

When the private mortgage insurers refused to pay claims on defaulted loans, the GSEs would then start to push the loans back to the lenders like Freedom Mortgage for reimbursement. And Stan and his team knew that the mortgage insurers would not pay out on their insurance, because they failed to pay a decade before. Remembering the metaphor of risk being a merry-go-round served Stan very well indeed.

In the late 1980s, Freedom Mortgage worked with a mortgage company called Green Tree, which was owned by Security Savings & Loan, a bank in the wholesale mortgage business. Security was eventually taken over by the Federal Deposit Insurance Corporation (FDIC) and Resolution Trust Corporation in 1991 and cost the deposit insurance fund $100 million because of loan losses and management fraud. Green Tree tried to make Freedom Mortgage repurchase loans that the agencies tried to make the repurchase. These were stated income or asset loans with little or no documentation compared to today's standards for fully documented or "full-doc" loans.

Freedom Mortgage ended up not having to repurchase most of the loans in question, but it was an important time for Stan as the relatively new owner of an independent mortgage bank. The pattern of behavior Freedom Mortgage and other lenders saw in the late 1980s and early 1990s, whereby the various banks and nonbanks in the chain of ownership tried to pass their responsibility for a loan to somebody else, informed their view of the future. Just as falling rates make mortgage volumes soar, rising defaults cause the GSEs to seek repurchase of loans and the mortgage insurers to renege on their promises to cover the cost of a default.

At that time, Fannie Mae was making banks repurchase loans that were sold into an agency called MBS. Then the banks sent the loan to the mortgage company, which then ultimately went back to the borrower. The banks would try to get the mortgage company to cover the loan, but Stan's classic response to the banks was simple and direct:

"You underwrote the loan. What do you want from me?"

The asset correction of the late 1980s and early 1990s was an extremely important learning experience for Stan and his colleagues at Freedom Mortgage. The fact that the GSEs were trying to make mortgage banks repurchase loans after the insurer declined to pay on the private mortgage insurance was an eye-opener, especially since by then Stan was involved with the GSEs in a variety of industry forums in Washington!

"That was a big warning: The GSEs and large banks are capable of asking people to repurchase loans—loans that are supposedly government guaranteed," Stan remembers. "I always told people that if we didn't have the credit approval authority, that saves us a lot of money. If we didn't actually underwrite the loan and make the final credit decision, then we should not be on the hook for the loan."

For Stan and Freedom Mortgage, the clear message from the subprime lending boom was that credit was important and for many reasons. There was always a division in the industry between credit and sales. Brokers did the originations and, for many lenders, were really an outsourced loan originator. Citibank and some of the S&Ls took that example to an extreme in wholesale lending, when they did all of the processing and underwriting, and used independent mortgage banks purely for acquiring leads. This allowed, in theory, for the brokers to originate more loans. But for Citibank, Security Savings & Loan, and later Countrywide, the wholesale mortgage model was a disaster.

Outsourcing was a widely heralded concept at that time, a way to reduce the cost of capital or so it seemed. For people working in the mortgage business, the opportunity was to slowly perform more and more of the tasks involved in the loan process, and using technology to gain operating leverage was an important goal. But for Stan, his fascination and curiosity about the details of manufacturing and eventually selling a mortgage to a bank or directly to institutional investors led him to learn every aspect of the transaction.

"You got paid a little more to do the processing and you got paid a little more to do the closing docs for the mortgage," Stan reminisces. "We got paid a little more if we warehoused the loan and a little more if we closed the loan in your name. We learned one piece of the puzzle at a time. We became proficient in sourcing, underwriting and closing the mortgage."

Working through the difficult period of the 1990s was a heck of a way for Stan and his colleagues to learn the business. It taught them that closing the loan and retaining control of the mortgage servicing asset was an important part of the business of mortgage banking *and* credit, a part historically controlled by banks. As Stan's understanding of the mortgage business grew, investing his cash into loan servicing as capital assets and focusing on credit made more and more sense and gave Freedom Mortgage more substance as a financial firm.

Stan and his team suspected that the boom in the early 2000s would end with a broad correction, much like the earlier boom ended in the late 1980s. They knew that the GSEs probably would experience problems with the private mortgage insurers and that the GSEs then would bury lenders in loan repurchase claims. As a result, Stan made the decision to look for a way to grow his government loan business with the FHA and Ginnie Mae and thereby diversify some of Freedom Mortgage's business risk away from the GSEs.

Irwin Financial Transforms Freedom Mortgage

The perfect opportunity finally arrived in 2004, when Stan heard about an opportunity involving the mortgage division of Irwin Financial, a Midwest commercial bank that already was a top ten Ginnie Mae issuer nationally. Stan engaged a veteran investment banker named Dale Kurland, who had worked at Bear Stearns for many years and developed a unique expertise in mortgage assets.

"Irwin was forced to sell their mortgage business because regulators thought that the bank owned too much mortgage servicing and servicing assets were on the outs with bank regulators because of interest rate volatility," Stan recalls of the Irwin transaction. "Dale had been at Bear Stearns for a number of years and she was buying and selling not only companies but also MSRs. There were a lot of very smart, interesting people at Bear Stearns in those days including Michael Nierenberg, Mary Hagerty, and Baron Silverstein. So we worked with Dale on the Irwin transaction and that began a very long relationship."

Freedom Mortgage buying Irwin was like the minnow swallowing a whale, but Freedom Mortgage eventually was selected as the buyer, and the deal closed two years later in 2006. For Stan, the Irwin transaction represented a big change, in terms of both the financial commitment and what the acquisition meant for Freedom Mortgage. Up to that point, Stan related, he was able to control the outcomes for Freedom Mortgage reasonably well. With the Irwin purchase, however, the business grew in terms of highly talented and experienced people and other assets that enabled the business to really take off. Stan recalls that period with pride:

"Early in the 2000s we had reached the point where we were getting better financing terms from the banks. We had amassed $20 million or so in net worth, which was a lot of money then. I was making decisions that were more 'should I' rather than 'could I' situations, which allowed me to mostly control the outcome. Most of my life I faced 'couldn't' and 'shouldn't' sort of situations, but then I did it anyway because I had nothing to lose. But buying Irwin was a big step for me and for Freedom Mortgage."

The Irwin Mortgage purchase took Stan across a threshold from being a small business that was very compact and personal to a medium-sized enterprise with hundreds of employees and a substantial business as a Ginnie Mae issuer. Through the painfully slow years of the late 1990s and the Russian debt default, Freedom Mortgage had been a small mortgage bank and survived by making loans that were sold to banks. But Stan would establish relationships with Bank Boston, and then J.P. Morgan Chase and KeyBank, allowing him to become a full-fledged mortgage banker rather than merely a loan broker. So when the Fed dropped interest rates after 9/11, Freedom Mortgage was nicely positioned to grow its lending and servicing portfolio.

Irwin had four mortgage production channels and a servicing group, which added enormous scale to Freedom Mortgage as a lender and eventually a loan servicer. This transformational transaction established Freedom Mortgage's position as one of the largest privately held mortgage companies in the nation. And Irwin had been involved in a number of exotic loan types like piggyback loans and even subprime lending, probably another reason that regulators wanted the bank to sell. Overnight, buying Irwin gave Stan a bigger, more experienced team of managers and a solid operating platform upon which to grow. Many of the managers from Irwin remained at Freedom Mortgage for many years thereafter, and some to this day.

Stan got some very talented people from Irwin who took on leadership roles at Freedom Mortgage as the years progressed. Freedom Mortgage acquired people and processes that were more from the world of banking than mortgage broker, enhancing Freedom Mortgage's internal systems and controls. Freedom Mortgage now had a team and infrastructure that looked like a bank and behaved like a bank on bank technology. And it gave Stan the ability to issue Ginnie Mae securities when the market for conventional loans became unattractive.

"When we acquired Irwin, I was upside down on the transaction and the cost of running a much larger company," Stan recalls. "For a couple of years, I was not sure whether the Irwin transaction was a good deal or not. But by the time we fought our way through 2008 and emerged on the other side, I knew we had made a very good deal for some very valuable people and assets."

Stan bought the loan production side of the Irwin business, while the servicing portfolio was sold to a company called New Century. That subprime lender and servicer would fail in 2007. New Century was acquired out of bankruptcy by a private-label mortgage issuer named Carrington, which grew that business into a successful lender and high-touch servicer of distressed private and government mortgages.

Carla Wise, who was the president of servicing at Freedom Mortgage until July 2020, spent decades at Irwin and worked her way up through every aspect of loan servicing and collections. Carla initially went to New Century with the Irwin team and ran that entire operation for eight years. She held senior management positions at New Century, IndyMac, Lehman Brothers, and Aurora Bank FSB. At IndyMac, Carla worked for J.K. Huey and Tony Ebers. Carla was one of first women in the mortgage industry to break through the glass ceiling and into upper management in terms of running an entire mortgage servicing business. She joined Freedom Mortgage in September 2012 to lead the next phase of the company's growth, namely, building an in-house servicing business.

Mike Patterson, now Chief Operating Officer at Freedom Mortgage, headed an important part of Irwin's loan production team working for Les Acree, who has also been with Freedom Mortgage since 2006 and initially headed wholesale and correspondent lending. Immediately after the Irwin transaction closed, Mike was tasked with running Freedom Mortgage's wholesale business and took on a big chunk of the responsibility for finance and capital markets within the company.

The acquisition of Irwin expanded Freedom Mortgage's geographic reach into the Southeast, Midwest, Arizona, and Florida, important additions that helped provide greater national coverage and therefore geographic diversification for the business. The big challenge of acquiring Irwin, however, was merging two significant teams together, teams that came from dramatically different experiences and cultures but had enormous potential to create value together.

Combining Irwin with Freedom Mortgage was a complex, lengthy process. Financially, Freedom Mortgage was still a small lender and had only started to accumulate significant capital and assets. Irwin was a large producer and a significant and respected player in the government loan market, which was a big reason for pursuing the acquisition. Stan said:

> "There certainly was a bit of culture shock. Irwin was the mortgage subsidiary of a commercial bank and was largely decentralized from bank management. Freedom Mortgage was an integrated, entrepreneurial company where producing mortgages was the one and only goal. The Irwin team had to suddenly deal with an intense, involved owner and chief executive that wanted to know and understand every single detail of the business."

During that time, Stan was very involved in the details of the business. How much profit did we make on a given loan? How much did that widget cost for operations? He constantly quizzed Mike Patterson and his colleagues, in part because he was learning from them. The melding of the cultures worked, however, and Stan quickly realized that with Irwin, he and Freedom Mortgage also acquired the nucleus of the experienced management team he had long wanted to build. Combined with his veteran sales and operations team, the Irwin purchase would enable Stan to shift from worrying about operations to thinking about strategy and what's around the corner.

It speaks well for Freedom Mortgage that years later, many of the senior leaders of the Irwin team—Carla, Mike, and Les Acree, and many others—are all still with the company in substantial management or advisory positions. All saw that Freedom Mortgage was very open to talented people who wanted to take ownership of significant parts of the business. And Stan quickly conceded to them responsibility for making Freedom Mortgage grow.

As is often the case in corporate combinations, many of the most important assets are not measured in dollars and cents. The human and financial assets gained through the Irwin transaction, and the change process that began in 2006 and has never really ended, positioned the firm for growth and stability over the next two decades. The Irwin transaction was also a big event for Stan as a manager and owner. He suddenly had an abundance of seasoned, competent managers who assumed that they had to take responsibility.

"We could no longer walk; we were running flat out," Stan says of the time of the Irwin acquisition. "I challenged the team to walk me through every single detail of every single process in every single department, but with the growing knowledge and expectation that they were doing a great job minding the details."

Stan found that he and his team had to learn together and manage an increasingly complex business together. Every day was an education. He had to now spend more time in Washington. And today, sometimes, he still asks that one-inch level questions as part of his role of risk manager. Together with strategy and vision, Stan maintains, the chief job of any executive is to manage risk. When the strategy is delivered to the tactical managers, a key part of implementation is managing the risks that come along on the merry-go-round.

A big challenge Stan faced to make his new colleagues from Irwin feel at home was the process of going from a regulated, bureaucratic commercial bank culture to a flatter organization where meetings were fewer and shorter and people were rewarded to take the strategy they agreed upon and show initiative in terms of making things happen. For many, Stan recalls proudly, within three months after the transaction closed, they understood that Freedom Mortgage was a place focused on doing business the right way.

"It probably took a year for many Irwin employees to understand the way a nonbank finance company operates," says Stan with considerable pride. "Freedom Mortgage still had very detailed strategy and tactical goals to measure success and avoid risk, but they communicated these tasks in a far more efficient and informal fashion."

"If we had meetings, for example, they were brief and to the point," Stan continued. "The culture of managing to profitability rather than quarterly earnings was a big change as well. Yet once we set the team from Irwin free to achieve, they became the core driver of Freedom Mortgage's growth thereafter and also our strength to navigate difficult markets."

But perhaps as much as acquiring talented people that would come to run much of the business day to day, the purchase of Irwin gave Stan Middleman the time and the opportunity to think about the future of his business and try to identify and understand approaching risks. In terms of the long-term growth of Freedom Mortgage, this was perhaps the most important and yet unrecognized asset from that transaction.

"Stan originally hired me to provide oversight of the Freedom Mortgage servicing book, which was relatively small and outsourced to subservicers," notes Carla Wise of those early years. "But Stan was already thinking about the next step. Within a few months of joining Freedom Mortgage, he was asking me to help build an in-house servicing business and he put out some big numbers for where he wanted the business to go. Stan is a visionary. He is always trying to think a couple of steps ahead, looking into the future to try and understand what is happening in our business."

Carla, Mike, and many other professionals at Freedom Mortgage had their choice of where to work in the world of housing finance, but they chose to work for Stan Middleman. This is not just a testament to Stan's ability to attract top people but also goes back to his personal challenge of creating a shared vision for his team. At the end of the day, the long tenure of many Freedom Mortgage employees provides a great endorsement of Stan's ability as a leader to attract and retain a quality team—a key quality of any successful entrepreneur.

CHAPTER 9

FINANCIAL CRISIS TO COVID-19

TIMELINE

2006 Freedom Mortgage withdraws from subprime and conventional lending

Completes Irwin Financial transaction

2007 Housing bubble bursts

New Century Financial fails

Market for subprime loans evaporates

FOMC slashes interest rates

2008 Great financial crisis unfolds

Fed announces quantitative easing

2010 Freedom Mortgage makes decision to grow government loans

Freedom Mortgage reaches 100,000 servicing customers

2012 Achieves first $1 billion month in loan originations

When Freedom Mortgage closed the acquisition of Irwin Mortgage Corporation's loan origination business in 2006 for $350 million, it ensured Freedom Mortgage's future as a government mortgage lender. Stan had qualified for an FHA license years earlier, but Irwin gave him access to experienced people and operational skills that Freedom

Mortgage lacked. Combined with a new relationship with J.P. Morgan Chase and eventually KeyBank for warehouse financing, Freedom Mortgage was prepared to grow to a new level.

Once the ink was dry, Freedom Mortgage had more than 2,000 employees in 150 offices nationwide. And as we discussed in the previous chapter, the Irwin transaction added many valuable people to the Freedom Mortgage team. Yet, despite the promise and excitement this transaction brought to Stan Middleman, within a year, the Freedom Mortgage team was in a five-year battle for survival.

"Freedom Mortgage has for years been a successful company, and Irwin Mortgage offered exceptionally strong platforms in retail, direct, wholesale and correspondent delivery channels. This acquisition will catapult Freedom Mortgage to a new level," Stan Middleman said of the transformational deal.[22] Yet, even as he celebrated a great win for Freedom Mortgage, the mortgage market was already showing very visible signs of stress that would lead to the financial crisis of 2008.

Freedom Mortgage and other mortgage lenders saw another six to nine months of strong lending volumes, but then things began to change fast and not in a good way. By March 2007, the market for all private mortgages, from subprime to Alt-A, showed definite signs of fatigue. Yet, this was not really a surprise to Stan.

As early as 2005, Freedom Mortgage's underwriters saw that the credit performance of the Alt-A product being sold to the GSEs by some lenders was significantly worse than other nonagency paper. The "mission critical" lending by the GSEs turned out to be some of the worst performing mortgage assets created during the 2000s, "toxic waste" in Wall Street parlance. The last pool of fifty-four Alt-A loans

---

22   Globe Newswire, "Freedom Mortgage Closes Deal to Acquire Irwin Production Platform," September 18, 2006, https://www.globenewswire.com/news-release/2006/09/18/348393/7352/en/Freedom-Mortgage-Closes-Deal-to-Acquire-Irwin-Production-Platform.html.

Freedom Mortgage sold to Fannie Mae, with recourse, in 2006 all came back via repurchase claims later. It was déjà vu all over again, to paraphrase Yogi Berra, but the Freedom Mortgage management team had already made the decision to step away from the Alt-A market. Stan said:

"At the time of the close of the Irwin acquisition, our volumes were running about half conventional and half government loans and Alt-A product that was being delivered to Fannie Mae and Freddie Mac. We were not selling to the New Centuries and other private players, but we were originating Alt-A specifically for what the GSEs were buying for their portfolios."

In a very real sense, Fannie and Freddie in the 2000s became the new takeout investor for below-prime, Alt-A loans. Just as the S&Ls and Citibank had done a decade before, the GSEs were the buyers of choice in the subprime market. In the early 2000s, the GSEs effectively took the place of Citibank in the late 1980s and early 1990s as the takeout for fringe mortgage products, the stuff most banks and even bond investors would not touch. After all, home values had been rising for almost a decade through into the 2000s, and much of the housing industry was dead. Most lenders felt pretty good about the credit of loans because the market had decided that property values only rise. The same people believed that interest rates would never go down. Yet, these optimistic assessments would be tested very severely.

The collapse in 2008 confirms the conclusion of Gretchen Morgenson and Joshua Rosner in their 2011 book *Reckless Endangerment*, which asserts that the risk taking of Fannie Mae and Freddie Mac was a major element in causing the housing bubble. This narrative may displease progressives who revere the GSEs as legacies of the New Deal, yet the overwhelming body of evidence is that Fannie Mae and Freddie Mac drove the subprime mortgage bubble—until the big banks literally pushed them out of the way in 2005. Near the end of the upward surge in the housing cycle and just before the visible bust began in 2007, Wall Street pushed the market share of the GSEs down to about 40 percent. But, by that time, Stan Middleman and his team had already stepped away from the GSEs and the banks.

Starting in 2003, the GSEs bought just about all of the Alt-A loan production in the United States, Middleman recalls. In fact, Fannie Mae and Freddie Mac loved the below-prime product and could not get enough of it. The GSEs bought the subprime loans to keep in portfolio because of the relatively high loan coupons. These were low doc products with pretty standard payment terms, but the extra yield made them attractive to the GSEs and investors—until these loans lost their luster in the credit crisis that began in 2007.

"By December of 2006, the secondary market for Alt-A loan product was deteriorating," recalls Freedom Mortgage's Chief Operating Officer Mike Patterson. "From bids of 104 earlier in the year to 102 and lower by December, it was clear that the subprime party was over. As Fannie Mae and Freddie Mac began to bid less aggressively for Alt-A product, other bidders soon noticed and also backed away from the secondary loan market."

Freedom Mortgage's lending volumes in 2006 included 60 percent conventional loans for Fannie and Freddie, 20 percent government loans sold into the Ginnie Mae market, and 20 percent Alt-A loans. But, by early 2007, Freedom Mortgage made the decision to stop originating both Alt-A and conventional loans altogether. By that February, Freedom Mortgage was underwriting 90 percent government loans and Ginnie Mae MBS.

"By July 2007, we were producing 100 percent government-insured loans," Stan relates about that time. "Call it looking around the corner or just plain luck, but in that scary summer of 2007 we were in pretty good shape compared to our competition."

Stan never allowed his firm to get into option ARMs or other more exotic mortgage products—just Alt-A product that the GSEs were willing to buy. Indeed, a whole market sector coalesced around the GSEs in the early 2000s as the takeout investors for subprime loans. The big banks and the GSEs like Fannie Mae and Freddie Mac were the chumps of the financial crisis of 2008 story. From 2004 onward, the GSEs were the biggest buyers of subprime mortgages followed by the likes of Citigroup, all of which ultimately collapsed as liquidity fled the market in 2007.

But operators like Stan Middleman and others weathered the storm by pivoting away from the Alt-A and conventional loan market early on and returning to the safety of the government-insured loan market and Ginnie Mae. Freedom Mortgage had to change to a new product mix, and the team executed this change in fine fashion albeit with some bumps along the way. Because Irwin had always been a strong player in the government-insured loan market, they could refocus on that market as other lenders literally disappeared. The fact that Freedom Mortgage's government loans had FHA insurance and that claims were being paid, even as the GSEs and Citigroup slid toward government takeovers, enabled Stan and his team to manage through the crisis.

By the end of 2007, Chuck Prince, Sanford Weill's handpicked successor at Citibank, was forced out following the disclosure of huge losses in Citibank's subprime mortgage portfolio. By the end of 2008 and into the early part of 2009, banks started to withdraw entirely from providing wholesale funding to the mortgage business, a decision many lenders would later regret. After acquiring Countrywide, Bank of America simply shut down the nation's largest correspondent and wholesale channels. Citibank, which had been a lead warehouse lender for Freedom Mortgage, dropped out of the mortgage finance space after the government takeover but continued to be an important partner for the company. It is a considerable testament to Stan and the Freedom Mortgage management team that banks continued to support the firm's credit needs long after other mortgage banks were cut off.

After 2008, J.P. Morgan Chase also withdrew from both correspondent lending and warehouse financing but did so in increments that allowed Freedom Mortgage to gradually shrink its syndicate. J.P. Morgan Chase had accumulated significant market share in originations and warehouse lending; thus, the decision to exit the residential mortgage market after 2008 was a big negative and caused significant liquidity problems for many firms. Say what you like about the risks of nonbanks, but systemic risk occurs when large commercial banks decide to cut off liquidity to a given asset class, a truth that would be proven years later.

Overnight, Stan and his team saw available funding sources disappear. Loan production volumes were not terrible, so Freedom Mortgage was able to make money. Yet, Stan and his team were forced to manage both a sharp decline in business, generally, and a cut in access to funding, which ultimately determines how many loans you can close every month. By late 2008 and early 2009, everyone in the bank mortgage warehouse funding world was backing away from smaller nonbank lenders, but Freedom Mortgage managed to survive the market firestorm and position the company for future growth in government loans.

By 2010, all of the big banks took a step back from the mortgage sector with the notable exception of market leader Wells Fargo, which supported the market in those difficult years after 2008. Lenders were very shy about taking mortgage risk, even on government-guaranteed collateral. By definition, the liquidity available to Freedom Mortgage and all other nonbank lenders fell dramatically.

Adding to the confusion was the collapse of Taylor, Bean & Whitaker, which experienced significant financial fraud and ceased operations in June 2009. The failures of Colonial Bank, one of the twenty-five largest banks in the United States at the time, and TBW, one of the largest privately held mortgage lending companies in the United States, caused enormous disruption outside the world of home mortgages. The GSEs had been aware of the fraud at TBW for years but chose to hide the mess rather than blow the whistle.[23] This added to the scope of the problem once the FDIC seized the insolvent bank. Ginnie Mae and the FHA ultimately were forced to act, seizing collateral to protect their agencies.

The TBW collapse further damaged the market for firms like Freedom Mortgage, putting their very existence at risk. Every single bank that was still willing to lend to independent mortgage companies put Freedom Mortgage even more under the microscope. Being a larger independent lender that was not a bank made Freedom Mortgage suspect. The near-collapse of Wachovia, coming on the heels of the September 2008 bankruptcy filing by the parent of Washington Mutual Bank, sent credit investors, lenders, and counterparties running for the door.

Fortunately, Freedom Mortgage was able to maintain its relationship with J.P. Morgan Chase far longer than many other mortgage banks, a fact that probably allowed Stan to manage through this crisis. In fact, even after J.P. Morgan Chase CEO Jamie Dimon made the decision to step away from the mortgage business in 2010, the bank

---

23   Tom Schoenberg, "Fannie Mae Officials Kept Quiet about Taylor Bean Mortgage Fraud," *Seattle Times*, July 15, 2011, https://www.seattletimes.com/business/real-estate/fannie-mae-officials-kept-quiet-about-taylor-bean-mortgage-fraud/.

gave Freedom Mortgage plenty of time to transition and even helped them to start relationships with other lenders.

"We ended up with a number of smaller warehouse lines from a group of regional banks which were more difficult to manage but at least allowed us to continue doing business," recalls Mike Patterson. "By engaging with our lenders and helping them understand the true risks in our business, which were both identifiable and entirely manageable, we pulled through this difficult period and emerged stronger as a company and a team."

Over the years, Freedom Mortgage had built a good reputation with lenders, and a number of them stayed with the company through the financial crisis. J.P. Morgan Chase eventually passed the warehouse loan business to Citibank, which had reentered the market for mortgage finance. It is notable that Citibank never pulled an existing warehouse line from commercial customers and never lost money on their secured financing business to firms like Freedom Mortgage. Citibank remained an important partner at a reduced level even following the government rescue. And a few years later, J.P. Morgan Chase again became a warehouse lender to Freedom Mortgage and has been an important partner since that time.

The period of market upheaval both before and after 2008 put a substantial strain on the company and its people. Freedom Mortgage was accustomed to moving forward but now was forced to cut back on head count and overhead and carefully select which loans they were going to fund and close.

True to Stan's prediction, by 2009, Fannie Mae and Freddie Mac already were pushing back supposedly defective loans for reimbursement, and all conventional lenders were in a very difficult spot. Bank of America ultimately ceased doing business with Fannie Mae in 2012 because of a dispute over repurchase claims by the GSE during that period.[24]

By the end of 2009, Freedom Mortgage shifted most of its business away from the GSEs and into the Ginnie Mae market. In fact, in 2010, 2011, and 2012, there were many months when Freedom Mortgage's volumes were mostly government guaranteed for FHA, Veterans Affairs (VA), or US Department of Agriculture (USDA) loan programs.

"The decision to acquire Irwin and the ability to originate government loans in our own name had saved the company quite literally, allowing Freedom Mortgage to avoid the fate that befell other independent lenders," recalls Stan. "Living in tomorrow literally kept the doors open at Freedom Mortgage at a time when many others faltered. And it was the execution by our growing team in the government loan space that enabled us to survive the storm and then grow strongly from that protected base."

In 2006, half of the mortgages originated in the United States were nonagency loans. Less than 40 percent were conventional mortgages, and less than 10 percent were government loans. In just two years, government loans had jumped to 20 percent of the total, and private, nonagency loans basically disappeared. By late 2010 and early 2011, Freedom Mortgage made the strategic decision to grow strongly despite the recession and leverage the relationship with Ginnie Mae. That decision would guide the firm's growth and development for the next decade and see Freedom Mortgage eventually become one of the largest government lenders in the United States.

---

24 Nelson D. Schwartz, "Bank of America Breaks with Fannie Mae," *The New York Times*, February 24, 2012, https://www.nytimes.com/2012/02/24/business/bank-of-america-breaks-with-fannie-mae.html.

"We had picked up some new financing lines in 2010," Stan recalls of that difficult period. "The senior leaders of Freedom Mortgage came together and made the decision to double down and get aggressive on price for government loans. We grew our wholesale channel and actually started up a correspondent channel the following year—this at a time when the mortgage sector was basically treading water in terms of volume growth."

Freedom Mortgage was one of the independent mortgage banks, such as Rocket (a.k.a. "Quicken"), Mr. Cooper, and Penny Mac, that helped grow the Ginnie Mae market to 20 percent overall share today. By 2010, Ted Tozer was head of Ginnie Mae and refocused the agency on raising the level of service to consumers and issuers. He saw clearly the need for the FHA/VA/USDA markets to help the US mortgage sector recover and grow even as the GSEs entered conservatorship.

Freedom Mortgage's opportunity in government lending more than a decade ago was sparked by the Irwin acquisition, but it also required a great deal of focus and attention to detail in order to be an efficient government lender and Ginnie Mae servicer as time progressed. Ted Tozer's leadership at Ginnie Mae enabled firms like Freedom Mortgage and many others to grow in the government space. In those difficult days, the FHA was literally the only market for smaller loans for first-time home buyers. Today, at over $2.5 trillion in Ginnie Mae securities, Tozer's vision has been rewarded, and the FHA/VA/USDA mortgage loan market now accounts for almost 20 percent of all US mortgages.

"In addition to merely focusing on growing our government loan volumes after the 2008 financial crisis, we also aggressively started to grow our portfolio of loans and particularly servicing assets," Stan says proudly. "We started to see that the relatively stable cash flows from your servicing book could offset the swings in income from lending in different economic environments. And we started to build our servicing portfolio and our government business. Before the 2008 financial crisis we were a lot like other mortgage companies, but after we made a conscious decision to retain loans and servicing assets, accumulate capital and thereby grow value within Freedom Mortgage, starting the next chapter of our development."

Boom to Blah

During and after the 2008 financial crisis, Stan's focus on looking forward to identify risks was put to its toughest test yet. Congress passed the Dodd-Frank legislation in 2010, and the mortgage industry staggered along for several years thereafter, through the 2012 National Mortgage Settlement and the creation of the Consumer Financial Protection Bureau (CFPB). This period featured years of political investigations, and abusive fines and penalties levied on an already badly damaged industry. Not surprisingly, the amount of credit available to the residential loan market declined for a number of years.

The period of the 2010s was a lot like the 1990s. Both periods featured falling home prices and falling credit allocation to the housing market, making it difficult for consumers to get a mortgage. This lack of financing activity was a reflection of the fact that home prices fell dramatically in the 1990s, leading to an equally sharp reduction in new home construction. The entire housing ecosystem of the 2000s came crashing down in 2007. Home prices fell but less than in the 1990s. Yet, the aftermath of 2008 went on for almost a decade of regulatory action, litigation, and a general malaise across the mortgage finance sector. The fact that the FOMC maintained a largely accommodative stance in terms of interest rates through this period did not seem to matter to housing.

Think about the fact that 2003 had been the peak of mortgage lending volumes in the early 2000s at almost $4 trillion in new mortgage loans. In 2005, the industry again rose above $3 trillion in production, yet, from that point, the more aggressive players, such as Country-wide and Washington Mutual, began to record *declining volumes*, a telltale sign that the credit cycle is maturing and the market is becoming exhausted. By 2008, the mortgage market's volumes fell to just $1.5 trillion in production, confirming the slump that began in 2005.

US home prices had started to decay in early 2007, but home prices would take many years to stabilize as millions of Americans faced foreclosure. Home prices nationally would not bottom out until January 2012 and then began a slow climb back up to the 2007 peak levels by the end of 2016.

Lending volumes remained weak during this whole period, but Freedom Mortgage and other government lenders were able to rebuild their origination business and also accumulate servicing assets that would become extremely valuable by the end of the decade. Stan's focus on "the asset," including both the loan and the servicing of the loan, would serve Freedom Mortgage very well and provide a solid capital base upon which to build a truly national lending business.

Lending volumes in the United States bottomed out in 2014, when total mortgage originations were just $1.2 trillion and the total amount of mortgage debt was running off rapidly. Yet, as had been the case in the 1990s, the gradual accumulation of demand from young families to buy a home soon began to push the loan volumes higher.

Home building in the United States began to collapse rather dramatically after 2006, falling from just shy of eight million new homes annually to less than two million by 2010.[25] New home building essentially limped along for half a decade, and even by 2020, new home construction remained below half of the 2006 peak levels. This was one of the reasons why home prices began to accelerate in 2016 and went parabolic after COVID-19 exploded in 2020, rising at double-digit annual rates.

Getting from the falling prices of the years immediately after 2008 to the soaring home prices a decade later required lenders to navigate the period of home foreclosures and nonperforming loans that forever changed the mortgage industry. Starting in 2009, when the US banking industry charged off tens of billions of dollars in delinquent loans, the industry experienced a period when many distress properties were trading far below the actual value of the asset, creating a feeding frenzy among investors and politicians alike. While the industry worked diligently to process the massive backlog of busted mortgages and abandoned homes, politicians took maximum advantage of the situation, demonizing the industry for essentially doing their jobs. The CFPB levied billions of dollars in fines against mortgage companies and forever changed the business.

By the middle of the decade of the 2010s, the market for private mortgage loans had disappeared, leaving the only alternative for borrowers above the size limit for conventional and government loans the bank market. While some hard money lenders continued to provide credit to owners of larger homes, the dynamic that supported a market where more than half of all loans were done without any government backing was gone. It would take years for nonbank issuers of larger mortgages, such as Redwood Trust, to rebuild that market

---

25   Karan Kaul, Laurie Goodman, and Michael Neal, "The Role of Single-Family Housing Production and Preservation in Addressing the Affordable Housing Supply Shortage," https://www.urban.org/research/publication/role-single-family-housing-production-and-preservation-addressing-affordable-housing-supply-shortage.

and, most important, the confidence of investors. Like the 1990s, the 2010s were a time of change and consolidation in the world of mortgage finance.

Change and Success

"Sometimes change is viewed as a dirty word, the enemy of us all, especially if you observe how people react to change," Stan reflected during an interview about the 2008 period. "They assume change will make everything worse, rather than simply different. But to the person who wants to see around corners, change is a given and really just another word for opportunity. Change is another tactic to exploit the possibilities in front of you, possibilities that sometimes change before your eyes. Change is not something we want to be afraid of, it's something we want to understand and embrace."

We all hear about companies being disruptors and others that weren't able to keep pace with the new environment, Stan observed during the interview. As the speed of technology moves faster, and faster, and faster, it becomes more difficult for leaders and businesses to adjust to that change. The ability to embrace change is one of the most valuable tools in our arsenals, Stan believes. Add to this challenge, however, the need to adapt to unanticipated risks and curves in the road that materialize unexpectedly. Stan said:

"In my experience, I've found that people who embrace change succeed and those who don't fail. Adapting to change is a skill set that needs to be practiced. Sometimes, you hear professional athletes talk about how the game slows down for them, even though, at different levels, the 'speed of the game' picks up. For those who become master of their sports see the game slow down. I think that's metaphorical, because the game doesn't actually slow down. Their capacity to understand what's happening around them speeds up. That's the critical understanding: if you can see change, you can deal with change."

If you can understand that you are using change as a tool to improve your situation, or to better take advantage of an opportunity, that's when change becomes an ally and not an enemy. If the people around you trust you enough to embrace the change that you bring to them, because you've built a history of credibility around change, Stan argues, they will climb aboard for the ride. Like Stan always says about interest rates: they can go up, go down, or stay the same. You need a plan for each eventuality.

"When you begin to implement change, you implement it in a methodical fashion that allows people to adjust," Stan relates when looking back at the decade of the 2010s. "In 2008, we had no choice but to change. That's critical so that people can see what's in it for them, because that's the underlying issue. Why should I change? What's in it for me?"

Based on decades of building his team at Freedom Mortgage, Stan appreciates that when you need to get other people to change, to alter the program in order to survive and grow, the fact that they are already accustomed to change is a huge asset. If they are not ready for change, if they are not used to changing, then they're going to spend more time asking that "why" question. They spend less time pursuing the goals and taking advantage of the opportunities that are in front of them.

Validating Stan's view of change as a constant in life is relatively easy. More often than not, success in business is about managing short-term risks while moving toward long-term goals. Tactics are as important as strategy. Change, in and of itself, really is a critical tool that has to be used correctly. It has to be practiced often, to the point where it becomes a conditioned part of your environment. People who deal with you in your environment have to understand it and appreciate it. Stan encountered many changes over three decades in business.

"We've talked about the coming and going of opportunity during the US Bicentennial in 1976, and how those changes, in a positive and in a negative way, impacted my ability to succeed as an entrepreneur. We talked about the Disco Deli and my earliest experience as a manager, both in terms of guiding a business and taking responsibility for other people. To this day, I still think about that night when the Calico Kitchen was robbed at gunpoint. My major worry as I laid face down on the floor was the safety of the people who worked for me."

The challenges that Stan faced early in his business career only became more complex as he rose to a position of leadership in the US mortgage industry. As Freedom Mortgage grew in size financially and in terms of the size and geographic reach of the team, Stan took on the responsibility for a growing family of people who depended upon him for their livelihoods just as he had done with his siblings, his own growing family, and the people who had worked for him in earlier days. The constant during this period was a focus on the details and an unwavering discipline to keep looking down the road for the next surprise.

One important milestone for Freedom Mortgage during the slow and difficult years of the 2010s was the arrival of another member of the Middleman family to the business. Michael Middleman had worked part time at Freedom Mortgage starting in his teens, working first in the most difficult as well as an essential part of the business, namely, the call center. In 2015, Michael joined the company full time after working at a major audit firm focusing on the valuation of structured securities. Stan Middleman had come to the mortgage industry starting from a career in sales and then learned operations and finally the investment side of mortgage lending. Michael came to the home lending business with a strong theoretical and practical grounding in both accounting and finance, including his father's favorite asset, the MSR.

"I worked in the business starting in high school, mostly during the summer," Michael reflected during a 2021 interview:

"I first started in the call center, making outbound calls to customers and prospects. Then I moved to postclosing and underwriting, so that I gained a broad familiarity and appreciation for the different pieces of the business. One of my older cousins, Randy Gersten, worked at Freedom Mortgage at the time. My goal was always to meet or exceed his level of work, which was a challenge but also a great source of motivation. We took paper loan applications over the phone all day long. My one goal was to have a higher stack of paper than Randy by the end of the day."

In those early days, Michael learned one of the key lessons of the mortgage industry, namely, that just because a customer signs a loan application does not necessarily mean that the loan is going to close. He worked as a loan officer one summer, generating an impressive number of leads and loan applications, but was later surprised to find that many of these promising opportunities had not materialized in a closed loan. Mortgage lenders, after all, only get paid if the loan closes.

When Michael graduated from college in 2008, he had first wanted to work in banking and the capital markets. Michael wanted to be his own man and make his way in the world by himself. He also shared his father's curiosity and wanted to learn all aspects of the world of banking and finance. His father had told Michael many times that accounting is the language of business and provides a solid foundation for understanding any industry as you move through your career.

Trading was Michael's first choice out of college. He spent several years working in the world of structured finance, including stints at major banks and audit firms. Michael quickly learned that the world of the investment banker is just as rewarding and also volatile as the world of mortgage finance. By 2014, however, he decided to join Freedom Mortgage full time and immerse himself in all of the myriad aspects of the world of mortgage lending, financing, and servicing.

> "I worked for other firms during college and in the years after graduation. When I graduated college, we were in the middle of a serious economic crisis and many of the firms I approached were downsizing. I took a job at a small auditor, earned my CPA, then took a position at Ernst & Young in the structured finance group. I was assigned a number of forensic audit assignments related to the aftermath of the mortgage crisis that were fascinating. After some great years at E&Y, I made the decision to join Freedom Mortgage full time. At the time, my main goal was to learn more about and add value to the family business."

Much of the work that Michael participated in while at E&Y echoed many of the cautionary comments that his father had made to the Freedom Mortgage team over the years, namely, that the more complex mortgage instruments ultimately hid a great deal of credit and market risk. Stan and some of his peers among today's largest nonbank lenders survived the 2008 crisis because they did not follow Bear, Stearns & Co., Lehman Brothers, and many other firms into the more reckless corners of the subprime sector.

During his time at E&Y helping to clean up the mortgage mess, Michael learned firsthand what happens when lenders and investors take their eye off the ball in terms of managing both credit and market risk. Michael not only learned how to approach new modeling tasks for securities that, in many cases, had never been properly assessed in terms of valuation and potential volatility but also began to work as a leader of some valuation tasks for complex securities. Default triggers were being tripped in many private mortgage securities during this time, but Wall Street was unprepared to do the analysis. As his father had done decades earlier, Michael began to learn that the secret to building a good team is to assemble good people, give them clear instructions and responsibility, and then manage the team to success by encouraging excellence and continuous growth and improvement.

One area of particular focus for Michael at the end of his time at E&Y was MSRs, an asset that the team at Freedom Mortgage led by Simon P.B. Aldrich, senior executive vice president, knows as well as any in the industry. Simon, who is considered one of the most astute buyers of MSRs in mortgage finance, is a great example of how Stan surrounded himself with industry leaders who knew and understood the mortgage industry, and its opportunities and risks.

"In my final year at E&Y, we built a group specifically focused on MSRs, an asset that few people understood," recalls Michael. "I was the MSR guy and it very quickly became an asset that many people wanted to learn about. I spent a great deal of time helping clients understand this very valuable asset. And I was often on the phone with my father, Simon, and our MSR team to understand what was happening in the market."

Part of Michael's interest in mortgage finance and MSRs was sparked naturally enough because his father was already one of the biggest players in the market for mortgage servicing assets. But working through the financial crisis and performing valuations on busted MBSs and MSR portfolios reinforced Michael's belief in the way that Freedom Mortgage views themselves first and foremost as a portfolio manager.

"Our main asset is the MSR," Michael relates:

"We create MSRs by making loans. We try to do so in such a way that we keep cost down and fill up our bucket in terms of capital. In the early days we only invested cash in MSRs, but by 2017, when the market was picking up, we added modest leverage. The key thing for me is keeping the portfolio management approach to our business. We have a view of the servicing asset and the valuation over time and through the economic cycle. We hedge the MSR with our new origination and recapture capabilities. If we can originate and acquire MSR below fair market value, and recapture our share of refinancings, we can take advantage of swings in interest rates and the lending market very effectively."

The Rebound

The 2010s were a decade of rising home prices. Valuations rose at first slowly around 2012, when home prices on a national basis bottomed out and then began to move higher at an accelerating rate. As the banks and private investors slowly cleared the market of distressed properties, properties in general started to rise after almost five years of asset price deflation. This period was different from the 1990s, however, because the rebound in housing markets was driven by older, more affluent households that focused on Southern and West Coast markets.

Communities like San Diego and San Francisco led the 20-City S&P/Cash Shiller Index by 2016, while New York and the Northeast lagged the national average because of high taxes and levels of regulation that made these states unattractive to investors. Fort Lauderdale, Florida, for example, was identified as the fastest-growing market between 2010 and 2019, according to Redfin, up 160 percent in that period.[26] Orlando and Miami rose by triple digits as well. During this same period, the value of US housing assets rose by $11 trillion, according to Zillow, to over $33 trillion.[27] One-fifth of this total value was accounted for by one state—California.

Although the increase in home prices gladdened the hearts of homeowners and lenders, for new families entering the mortgage market, this was a daunting prospect. Most of the increase in value for US housing assets over the past decade came about because of rising prices for existing homes, not from building new homes. This is a fundamental difference between the 2000s housing boom and the decade that followed. Indeed, as this book was finalized in the middle of 2023, home prices were still rising despite sharply higher levels of interest rates.

"We reached 65 percent homeownership a decade after the great financial crisis, but the steady increase in the cost of buying a home makes me concerned that we could see that figure fall down into the 50 percent range over time," Stan observed in a 2022 interview. "High inflation and home prices seem to be here to stay, so I worry a bit that we may become more and more a nation of renters. The involvement of large investors in the housing market is not making prices comes down."

Like the 1990s, the 2010s represented a period of financial resolution and dislocation for millions of consumers, a fact that contributed to the sluggish economy and slow home price appreciation. Most home buyers in the 2010s were older Americans as opposed to millennials, a group that would participate in greater numbers as the

---

26   Redfin.com, "Florida Housing Market Overview," accessed September 2023, https://www.redfin.com/state/Florida/housing-market.

27   Treh Manhertz, "Recovery Riches: The U.S. Housing Market Gained $11 Trillion in Value in the 2010s," Zillow.com, January 16, 2020, https://www.zillow.com/research/us-total-housing-value-2019-26369/.

decade neared an end. When the recovery began to take hold and accelerate in the later years of the decade, however, the size and rate of increase in demand for homes and credit took many analysts by surprise after years of sluggish but stable growth.

"The US economy is still in the longest expansion on record, more than 126 months and counting," reported the Bureau of Labor Statistics. "The 2010s were the first decade without a recession since record-keeping began in the 1850s, and the official unemployment rate hovers at a fifty-year low."[28] Interest rates and reported inflation remained low through the decade, even as the FOMC struggled to make inflation rise—a fatal mistake that would come back to haunt the US central bank in 2022 when inflation soared to a fifty-year high.

"If we ended up with a slightly higher interest rate environment, it would actually be a plus for society's point of view and the Fed's point of view," Treasury secretary Janet Yellen said in a *Bloomberg News* interview on June 7, 2021. "We've been fighting inflation that's too low and interest rates that are too low now for a decade."[29]

One of the reasons often cited for the poor performance of the housing sector in the 2010s was the lack of new home building. In the 2010s, new construction started for 9.8 million new housing units in the United States, compared to 15.4 million units in the roaring 2000s and 13.7 million units in the 1990s.[30] But as Stan

28 Sean M. Smith, Roxanna Edwards, and Hao C. Duong, "Unemployment Rises in 2020, as the Country Battles the COVID-19 Pandemic," US Bureau of Labor Statistics, June 2021, https://www.bls.gov/opub/mlr/2021/article/unemployment-rises-in-2020-as-the-country-battles-the-covid-19-pandemic.htm.

29 Saleha Mohsin, "Yellen Says Higher Interest Rates Would Be 'Plus' for U.S., Fed," Bloomberg News, June 6, 2021, https://www.bloomberg.com/news/articles/2021-06-06/yellen-says-higher-interest-rates-would-be-plus-for-u-s-fed.

30 Victoria Stilwell, "Housing Starts in U.S. Surge to Second-Highest Level since 2007," Bloomberg News, July 17, 2015, https://www.bloomberg.com/news/articles/2015-07-17/housing-starts-in-u-s-climb-on-surge-in-apartment-building.

likes to remind the author, the dearth of home building in the 1990s actually started with the Resolution Trust Corporation and the S&L bust in the 1980s; thus, the current slump in home building is not so remarkable.

"It always takes a long time for home building to catch up with supply after a major economic correction such as 2008," Stan argues. "Eventually, we will see supply catch up with demand, but the big difference this time is home prices and affordability. That is what is different about the current cycle. It always takes a long time between boom cycles because home prices tend to rise quickly as interest rates fall. In 2002 and 2003, for example, interest rates fell after 9/11, and the mortgage market surged in terms of production volumes and home prices into 2005."

Historically, the supply of new homes has been constrained by government regulation, but today land prices and building costs are even more formidable barriers. Zoning restrictions are some of the chief obstacles to building more affordable housing, particularly the more expensive urban areas. But the key question that few seem to ask is whether any degree of liberalization of housing policies would really make expensive cities, such as New York, Miami, or San Francisco, affordable for people of average means. Soaring land prices and construction costs seem to already have precluded that outcome.

Total 1-4 family residential mortgages outstanding in the United States bottomed on Q3 of 2015 below $10 trillion and then began slowly to climb along with home prices for the rest of the decade and reached $11.5 trillion by the first quarter of 2020. Mortgage industry volumes and profits were not impressive by historical standards, but that was about to change.

In fact, 2018 was one of the toughest years for the residential mortgage industry in the 2010s, with originations below $2 trillion and average profit per loan of just 14bp, according to the MBA Performance Report.[31]

It says something about how Stan thinks about his duty to serve consumers that in 2018, he was talking about helping homeowners pay off the mortgage faster. "In my view, the best mortgage is no mortgage. People should invest in their home, not in their home financing," Stan said in a December 2018 interview with *National Mortgage News*.

In 2019, production profits rose to 58bp, a good year with $2.7 trillion in new mortgages produced. But the steady improvement of the 2010s was about to be rendered almost irrelevant by COVID-19, the response by the Fed and Congress, and the incredible effort from the private industry and the government to deal with the pandemic over the next two years.

The COVID-19 Shock

"I joined Freedom Mortgage in March of 2020, literally a few weeks before the COVID pandemic started and the whole industry began to formulate a response," recalls Gregory Middleman, Stan's younger son, who focused first on the firm's growing technology needs.

"In a matter of days, we had to figure out how to manage our existing team, hire new associates, and support all of this activity remotely. I literally hired and managed a new technology team and did not meet most of them for a year. It was an extraordinary operational effort, but also a great success for Freedom Mortgage and the mortgage industry."

---

31   Mortgage Bankers Association, "Quarterly MBortgage Ankers Performance Report: Q1 2021," accessed September 2023, www.mba.org/docs/default-source/research-and-forecasts/res-sample-documents/q1_2018_mbas_quarterly_mortgage_bankers_performance_report-sample.pdf.

After a trial by fire in 2020 during the COVID-19 pandemic and the industry lending boom that followed, Greg's duties have grown to include the firm's correspondent lending division with responsibility for loan pricing and counterparty risk. As with his brother Michael, Greg is very focused on buying loans and mortgage servicing assets from the firm's correspondents as well as through an initiative called Freedom Mortgage Exchange, a platform where a number of buyers acquire MSRs.

"We took all of our relationships with hundreds of correspondent firms and added value for them by bringing other buyers to the table as well," Greg described in an interview. "Obviously the flow of business has slowed over the past couple of years. Our philosophy is that we are not going to buy market share or bid for business just for the sake of doing loans. We like to let the markets tell us how to respond when it comes to loan originations."

With the sale of RoundPoint Mortgage, Freedom Mortgage exited the retail channel and focused on correspondent as the largest volume channel. Of note, Greg joined Freedom Mortgage just as lending volumes were surging, but so too were the numbers of consumers who needed help. The operations team at Freedom Mortgage and other financial firms came to grips with the practical aspects of managing through COVID-19 and, at the same time, provided enhanced levels of service to consumers experiencing financial hardship.

Also in 2020, Greg and Michael witnessed the largest single market intervention by the US central banks. As COVID-19 caused huge disruptions across the economy, the Fed was busily pushing down the cost of credit for residential mortgages by several percentage points, causing a huge surge in mortgage production and demand for homes that took the industry up sharply to just shy of $5 trillion in volume in 2020. This was the largest single year of loan production since the mid-2000s, when Countrywide and Wells Fargo controlled huge chunks of the lending and servicing market.

At first, the Fed dropped interest rates in 2019 but then really stepped on the gas at the end of March 2020 with vast open market operations in response to COVID-19. The Federal Reserve Bank of New York bought most of the production of government and agency mortgage bonds for the next two years. The mortgage industry went from famine to feast, from a world of low double-digit production profits to record triple-digit margins of almost 160bp in that year. Profits in 2020 were more than twice the industry average profit tracked by the Mortgage Bankers Association (MBA).

"In other words, mortgage lending profit margins in 2020 were an astounding 262 percent of the historic average, and still 133 percent of it in 2021," notes former Freddie Mac president Don Layton.[32] "Even in a highly cyclical industry, that's an extraordinary increase during the dislocations of the pandemic."

Unfortunately, while 2020 and 2021 were extraordinary years for the mortgage industry, the period that followed in 2022 and beyond would be equally terrible in terms of falling volumes and profitability for most independent mortgage banks. After spending several years in Freedom Mortgage's correspondent unit, Greg sees a period of industry consolidation ahead:

> "Many of our customers did incredibly well in 2020 and 2021, but by mid-2023 80 percent of those customers were losing money every month. Things improved a little in the summer of 2023, but even the firms that make

---

32 Don Layton, "The Policymaking Implications of Record-High Mortgage Origination Profits during the Pandemic," Joint Center for Housing Studies of Harvard University, May 2, 2022, www.jchs.harvard.edu/blog/policymaking-implications-record-high-mortgage-origination-profits-during-pandemic.

money are just barely moving the needle. The lenders that are doing well are those with large servicing books, but even those are tending to be sellers of servicing and we are buyers. Over time, we see a lot of smaller lenders exiting the industry. We could see the larger players all double or triple in size."

Of note, Greg reported that Freedom Mortgage was doing a fair amount of conventional loans in 2023 but loans with average 60 percent LTV ratios and FICO scores in the low 700s. These are loans that are unlikely to face foreclosure or repurchase claims from Fannie Mae and Freddie Mac when the housing market reaches that inevitable correction. The impact of the volatility seen in the credit markets in recent years is that it is incredibly hard for young entrepreneurs wanting to be like Stan Middleman to start a new mortgage firm today.

Neither has market volatility helped homeownership. The impact of COVID-19 and the official response on home affordability were devastating for younger families, one reason that Stan comes back again and again to the basic issue of making housing accessible. Even after two years of interest rate increases by the Fed, home prices continued to rise through 2023. One way to observe this process of soaring prices reducing affordability was the steady movement of borrowers out of the government loan market into the conventional market, a function of steadily rising home prices and equally steady reduction in LTV ratios.

Simply stated, home prices don't always go up. As the price of the house rises, the apparent level of indebtedness falls, but when the home price declines precipitously, the loan can become underwater with no remaining equity in the home.

"As properties go up in value, you have a credit migration where borrowers refinance from a government loan into a conventional loan, lose the mortgage insurance, and lower their monthly payment," Stan observes. "They pick up a point of savings because the house is worth more, but the borrower is the same. In theory the risk of the loan has been reduced, but that view depends fundamentally where we are in the interest rate cycle. When prices correct, that loan will no longer seem so low risk."

As Stan likes to explain it, the loan is of a fixed nature, but the economic cycle is variable. Those two things don't play well together in the financial sandbox. This is why as the enormous crisis from COVID-19 was abating in 2021, Stan and Freedom Mortgage were already moving to manage their activity in the conventional market to preclude loan repurchase claims from the GSEs years hence. At the time, there were many lenders that were seeking to maximize their production in conventional loans for Fannie Mae and Freddie Mac, just like the Alt-A lenders that sold subprime loans to the GSEs right up until the correction in 2008. But then things changed, as Stan likes to say.

CHAPTER 10

TURNING THE NEXT CORNER

TIMELINE

2013 Cherry Hill Mortgage REIT IPO announced

Freedom Mortgage reaches 200,000 servicing customers,

$40 billion in revenue

2015 Anniversary of twenty-five years since founding of Freedom Mortgage

Head count grows to over three thousand employees

Recognized as #1 FHA lender in the United States with $3 billion/month

in new loans

2018 *Wall Street Journal* profile: "The New Mortgage Kings: They're Not Banks"

by Cristina Rexode and AnnaMaria Andriotis

2019 Freedom Mortgage taps the debt markets to raise over $1 billion

in permanent capital

Completes merger with RoundPoint Mortgage, bringing 370,000 new

customers and putting Freedom Mortgage among top ten servicers

2020 Freedom Mortgage reaches thirtieth year, sets records in new loan origina-

tions while assisting tens of thousands of consumers dealing with COVID-19

2021 FOMC begins to raise interest rates

2023 Interest rates on thirty-year mortgages reach 8 percent

"Addressing a gathering of mortgage executives a few years ago, Freedom Mortgage CEO Stan Middleman made a blunt assertion," *National Mortgage Professional* proclaimed in 2018: "There are only two ways to make more money in mortgages: create more production, or take on more risk. For mortgage brokers who are staring in the face of another year of disappearing originations, Option 2 may be the only real option at all."[33]

In writing this biography of Stan Middleman, we've had many opportunities to talk about his outlook for the mortgage industry and the US economy going forward for the balance of the decade. As usual, he was not lacking for opinions or for carefully considered perspectives on what lies ahead in terms of interest rates or housing prices. And as we've discussed in the previous chapters, Stan is not afraid to adjust the timing of his long-term outlook to reflect changes in how the economy and interest rates are unfolding in the wake of COVID-19 and related problems such as inflation. As much as entrepreneurs like Stan try to plan for the long term, a great deal of success in business comes down to tactical considerations.

"We're coming through a period where interest rates are rising, mortgage originations have plummeted, and the value of mortgage servicing assets have risen, which is proof of concept for how we built our business," Stan observed in August 2023. "When one opportunity is reduced, another opportunity presents itself. That goes to planning by our team. That didn't happen by mistake or because we were lucky. Our business is interest rate sensitive. So, there are only three possible outcomes: interest rates go up, go down, or stay the same. And we were comfortable with all three scenarios and remain so."

---

33   Katie Jensen, "Only Risk Will Lead to Reward," National Mortgage Professional, accessed February 2024, https://nationalmortgageprofessional.com/news/only-risk-will-lead-reward.

In the first quarter of 2023, Americans saw three large bank failures—Silicon Valley, Signature Bank of New York, and First Republic. To Stan, this was clear evidence that markets and regulators were not prepared for the possible outcomes, especially as the Federal Reserve had moved interest rates dramatically higher over the previous year. Silicon Valley Bank and Signature Bank, were borrowing short and lending or investing long, Stan argues, making problems inevitable.

The net result was a liquidity crisis, when consumers suddenly moved their deposits at a speed that shocked bank managers and regulators. The big question, of course, is why no federal bank regulators noticed that Silicon Valley Bank had 40 percent of its assets in MBSs. In effect, Silicon Valley Bank was dead months before the bank collapsed into the arms of the FDIC.

"Consumers are easily swayed by influencers," Stan says. "When the private equity firms that kept corporate funds at Silicon Valley moved their money out, and then told their clients to also get out, the result was a run. Information, true or imagined, can move through society rapidly and result in the failure of several banks. Even with the many management errors, the fact of consumers moving their money in a matter of days or hours made the result inevitable."

One thing that the failure of all three large banks in 2023 illustrated is that technology allows consumers to move quickly, but technology cannot address affordability for young families. Stan worries more and more about homeownership and how this revered American institution will survive in the years and decades ahead, especially with inflation pushing the American dream further and further beyond the grasp of so many people.

The home price inflation engineered by the Federal Reserve during the response to COVID-19 seems to be permanent, unless and until we actually see a home price correction in the years ahead. And that is precisely what Stan believes will occur, as we discuss later in the chapter. But his view of the future continues to be informed by Stan's curiosity, his relentless desire to understand how the merry-go-round of risk has changed in the second decade of the twenty-first century.

One example of this evolution in the thinking of Stan and his team at Freedom Mortgage is their focus on acquiring servicing assets even as prices for MSRs have risen. "I told my team to take an aggressive stance on MSRs because investors and regulators still don't understand the potential profits in servicing through the economic cycle. That MSR that we seemingly pay up to buy today will pay us three or four times in return as we refinance that customer, perhaps multiple times."

The view of Stan and his colleagues at Freedom Mortgage on the inherent value of the mortgage servicing assets reflects a nuanced perspective that includes factors like the value of escrow balances on Ginnie Mae compared to conventional loans or the option value of being able to refinance a borrower into a lower-cost mortgage multiple times. Valuation models used by analysis shops and regulators do not include these factors in the assessment of fair value of the MSR, but Stan is constantly thinking about the overall return on the MSR in a given interest rate environment.

"We are going to get paid on that MSR over and over again in better times for serving that customer that we acquire in difficult market conditions," Stan argues. "The secret is to plan your investment strategy and liquidity so that you can take advantage of the opportunity. You have to skate to where the puck is going, not where it is or was."

Another illustration of Stan's good distance vision came in 2018, when he told the audience at the Information Management Network's (IMN) Annual Mortgage Servicing Rights (MSR) conference in New York City that there was trouble coming. Mortgage rate volatility, which was largely absent for many years, will be more of a concern in 2018, said Stan Middleman. "Hedging is really important in this part of the cycle" as a result, he told the audience of fellow mortgage bankers.

At the end of 2018, the money markets seized up, and the FOMC began a period of extraordinary open market operations that would forever change the US housing market. Chief among these changes was the inflation of home prices and the erosion of affordability for millions of American families. But the Fed's actions before and during COVID-19 would also change how Stan viewed the mortgage market as the pandemic began to fade from memory.

Today and Tomorrow

One of the rules this author has followed in three decades as a banker is to look at the obvious, mostly because so many people don't do that and assume that *somebody else* is managing the risk. As we've learned in our discussions with Stan, living in tomorrow requires that you concern yourself more with others than yourself. By doing this, you inform your perspective and ultimately serve your interests as well.

Sensitivity to what is going on around you, with your customers, your team, and your family, remains the core philosophy for Stan Middleman in his fourth decade operating Freedom Mortgage. This core discipline helped Stan and his team survive the subprime crisis of 2008 and the liquidity crises a decade later starting in 2018. The increased economic and political volatility of recent years, no surprise, has affected key factors such as employment and interest rates.

Stan talks about the art of managing the resources, people, and capital in a business, which is a practical and immediate concern. But we also need to think about tomorrow, both tactically and strategically, to avoid potentially fatal pitfalls, Stan believes strongly. This is especially true in the wake of the COVID-19 crisis, an outsized event few predicted. Stan and other business leaders were compelled to throw away the proverbial playbook and create a new way for people to work and live from home, all the while scaling the business to help COVID-19 victims and handle record production volumes.

"As the aftermath of the COVID-19 outbreak continues to unfold, civic and business leaders are being forced to think about society and people in an entirely new way," Stan observed in 2022 as interest rates rose and the mortgage industry downsized in response. "And change is the toughest thing for people to do."

One fascinating aspect about Stan is that his focus and energy on looking ahead remain undiminished as does his hunger for information and perspectives. As he did years ago first starting in the world of business, Stan continues to test and modify his way of thinking, not so much about what will happen next but in terms of the timing and magnitude of the changes.

He remains committed to the idea that the essential quality of a good manager is to constantly be testing what you think that you know in light of the latest information. What may have been a solid view about staffing or facilities last week can be rendered obsolete in a matter of weeks because of external events like COVID.

"You have to vet your theory and make sure that it's a good idea and bounce it off people," Stan reflected years before, when we spoke about his early business ventures. "You must get a wide range of consensus approval that you're thinking about the deeper future the right way. That this event follows this action, and that follows that, so that you know that when the economy is down, it's going to be followed by the economy rising, it's going to be followed by this amount of inflation, it's going to be followed by that amount of employment growth. It's going to be followed by so much real estate availability. It's going to be followed by that much demand for your product."

All of these things are factors when thinking about tomorrow, Stan believes. It's not simple, it's not fast, and it's not easy. However, it is necessary, he believes, to try to think about key variables like employment and interest rates. The greatest error of all is not being wrong about what you think today but to not take the risk of thinking about what happens tomorrow. It's not having a thought about tomorrow and having that thought evolve.

You don't need to be right, Stan insists, but you just have to have a point of view, and then that point of view evolves through your awareness and sensitivity based on change in the environment. Massive changes like the COVID-19 virus show how fragile our assumptions can be about basic pieces of our business.

"If we could predict the future precisely, we would do that," Stan says of management. "But that hasn't really happened. Whatever is coming doesn't happen on this specific date, at that time, this will happen. That's not what I'm talking about. I'm not talking about seeing the future in a precise 'this event will occur' sort of terms. Rather, I think that the movement along the timeline will likely do this, it will likely do that, it will likely do the other thing. You evolve your view of tomorrow as we move through time, a difficult but necessary discipline for any manager."

One area where Stan and his team at Freedom Mortgage certainly excelled was in preparing for operational risk events such as COVID-19, among the most important and still not fully understood challenges to face the residential mortgage industry in many years. By being overprepared for disaster recovery, Freedom Mortgage was able to roll out and execute a plan for the entire company to support working from home for thousands of people and implement this change seamlessly while increasing head count by 50 percent in the process. Between 2020 and 2022, Americans survived COVID-19 and, in the process, became a society that works from home. In March 2020, 98 percent of employees at Freedom Mortgage came to the office. Two years later, 98 percent of the company worked remotely and showed no desire to return to the old pattern.

"Our IT group at Freedom Mortgage rose to the occasion and were really very effective in getting people to work from home," Stan recalls with considerable satisfaction.

> Even in India we got all of our outsourced partners working from home. We had been stockpiling PCs and other gear for months because our IT group and our risk functions saw the potential for a serious disruption in our business, so we were prepared. For example, starting in 2019 everybody in the company that got a computer received a laptop. We looked around the corner and saw a potential operational challenge in terms of hurricanes or other weather events, and we prepared. Little did we know that the disaster recovery plan that was intended for a specific business interruption for a limited period in a specific region of the country would be rolled out on a national and permanent basis! I am so very pleased and proud of the way our operations and IT people at Freedom Mortgage responded to the lockdowns caused by the COVID-19 pandemic.

During the early days of COVID-19, Stan Middleman and all of the leaders in the mortgage industry experienced a role change, from leader, strategist, and tactician primarily concerned with business issues to an outward-facing communicator and purveyor of hope and encouragement. Stan and his executive team immediately had to take on the new role of cheerleader and facilitator, giving employees working remotely for the first time an additional degree of attention and encouragement.

Stan's role during COVID-19 was a combination of psychologist and father figure, or grandfather, Stan said during a discussion of that period:

"I was a motivator and supporter, but at the same time did a lot of listening. The team told us what they needed to make the transition to work from home. Our IT and operations teams took that information and responded with flexibility and imagination. The whole company came together to deal with the challenge of COVID-19, just as organizations did around the country. But more, our people actually grew, they emerged from the routine we all had known, and they stepped up in an amazing way to embrace change. Watching our people respond to COVID-19 in 2020 is one of the proudest moments in my years at Freedom Mortgage."

There is a lot of debate among economists whether or not the FOMC should have acted aggressively in 2020 and purchased trillions of dollars in Treasury bills and MBSs, but the fact is that the liquidity that was created by the mortgage industry by refinancing homes also provided the cash to deal with loan forbearance for those people who could not pay.

By driving mortgage interest rates down below 3 percent, the Fed created a cushion of money that essentially kept America out of a 1930s-style debt deflation, a fact that figures very much into the mind of Stan Middleman and other industry leaders. Whether the Fed understood that this was going to happen is a matter for the history books, but the money was there, and America avoided a very nasty economic contraction in 2020–2021.

There was a certain level of panic in the streets in the first quarter of 2020, much of which was unjustified, Stan recalls of that time. A lot of people thought they had a problem, but then the Fed started buying securities aggressively, adding trillions in cash to the markets in a matter of weeks. That was all that Stan and other leaders of the mortgage industry needed to see from Washington in order to focus on helping people though COVID-19. By the Fed taking a page out of the existing playbook and buying MBS, they gave the industry the wherewithal to focus on COVID-19 and make mortgage payments for millions of people. Ultimately, after about a month of uncertainty, we all got on the same page, and no one's worst fears were realized.

Freedom Mortgage went on to have a record year in 2020, in part because Stan and his team were already starting to prepare for an eventual reduction in interest rates. They did not expect the Fed to push down interest rates as quickly and as far as ultimately occurred, but when the volumes started to spike in the second quarter of 2020, Freedom Mortgage was ready to ramp up production. They had already started to increase head count in the middle of 2019 and were still building when COVID-19 hit in March 2020. As in past cycles, Stan was looking for unemployment to rise and gross domestic product (GDP) to fall, which signals a down cycle in rates and an upswing in mortgage production. And he was so right.

One of the many ironies of the COVID-19 pandemic was that sending everyone home to work freed mortgage firms like Freedom Mortgage from the need to provide physical office space, parking, and the other overhead of a traditional office environment. This allowed the housing finance sector to quickly expand head count and operational capability even as it was shouldering the burden of supporting employees working remotely. In many respects for Freedom Mortgage and other mortgage lenders, 2021 was a repeat of 2020, although the record gain-on-sale margins seen in that year were already starting to recede. By 2022, the industry was starting to return to normal in a sense but more quickly than in past cycles. And now interest rates were rising significantly for the first time in many years.

COVID-19 and Shared Vision

What is fascinating about Stan's view of housing is that after three decades owning and managing a mortgage company, he continues to employ the basic guideposts of interest rates and employment to inform his business outlook. He adjusts his strategy and perspective to account for technological changes, political shifts, and the impact of the Fed. The order of the risk factors changes in each period, but the risks are basically the same. The relative simplicity and also the clarity that this approach brings to Stan's viewpoint enable him to guide his organization through some of the most volatile market conditions seen in the past century. It is the speed of change as much as the size of the change that most challenges the operators of finance companies in mortgages and other sectors. In order to see incoming risks, your time to understand and respond to change is ever shorter.

Regardless of the economic environment, your ability to manage employees, or the size of your organization down to your current cash flows, is crucial to survival in the mortgage industry, Stan argues, especially in 2022. You start with a particular issue but must understand the impact of that issue throughout your organization. The mortgage industry met historic levels of demand for handling distressed mortgages as a result of the COVID-19 lockdown, but by 2022, mortgage lenders were dealing with equally large-scale decreases in volumes across the mortgage finance sector. As in the 1990s and 2008, many thousands of people were put out of work and, in many cases, permanently lost their livelihoods in the real estate sector as a result of sharply higher interest rates.

With millions of Americans seeking to defer mortgage payments during the COVID-19 lockdowns, the mortgage industry was forced to suddenly increase head count and other resources to deal with the tidal wave of customers seeking help—even as Stan sent all of Freedom Mortgage's employees home! Prior to COVID-19, effective managers had to adjust for rising or falling volumes. But managers in the mortgage business also must be able to have the right staff on hand to scale up, to onboard large quantities of people and implement resources in an environment of growing volumes. COVID-19 stretched the industry's resources, but many thousands of professionals who work in housing finance got the job done and proved the ability to be flexible and innovative during a time of great stress.

"The ability to manage staffing and related resources is a critical capability and always has been, but 2022 has set a new standard for adjusting expenses in a time of rapidly falling volumes," Stan observed in the middle of that year. "Having flexibility in your workforce, and access to personnel and employees or technology in lieu of personnel and employees, is an incredibly important capability because you have to leverage the implementation and execution of your plan, which typically employs the factors of production, capital facilities, and people. In the world of consumer finance, people are the most important part of that equation."

Of course, the other piece of the management puzzle Stan loves to talk about is facilities. In a people-intensive, scaling business like consumer finance, you have to make sure that you have enough facility and excess capacity but not too much. In the first quarter of

2022, many mortgage companies saw the cost of producing loans rise above production revenues because some organizations failed to be sensitive to their surroundings in terms of the economy, the Fed, and the outlook for interest rates. The better managed firms in the industry started decreasing overhead costs in mid-2021, when volumes and loan pricing were both starting to decline rapidly. Yet, many people in the world of finance outside of the mortgage industry were caught by surprise.

"You want to make sure that you are not dragged under by the weight of the cost of carrying of excess capacity," Stan recalls as he discussed three decades of ebb and flow in the world of mortgage lending volumes. We learned earlier how Stan was forced to downsize his firm in the 1990s, losing many valued colleagues who were an important part of Freedom Mortgage's business. But Stan never forgot those hard lessons about the iron rule of the mortgage business, namely, the strong correlation between interest rates, employment, and profitability.

"Managing expenses has always been my first responsibility because of the changeable nature of consumer lending," Stan says.

> With COVID-19, however, the world was turned on its head and sent everyone home. Suddenly we have empty buildings and the need to support operations for thousands of people working from home. Ten years before, we could never have accomplished this enormous feat. But in 2020, thanks to people and technology, we were able to get it done and grow capacity at the same time. As we've discussed, things change, sometimes in ways we cannot anticipate. Indeed, it's making me rethink whether or not I need all these office buildings!

Of course, the answer is yes, we still need offices and facilities, but COVID-19 has made us think about flexibility in terms of work in an important and positive way.

Sometimes an opportunity or a challenge is small, or sometimes that opportunity is larger. Sometimes it requires more people, but sometimes it requires less people. But at the end of the day, as another part of living in tomorrow, you have to be looking out four, five, and six years ahead in terms of capital, people, and facilities to meet that level of business. With COVID-19, Stan and Freedom Mortgage were forced to embrace personal and collective flexibility as a key operating principle, something that is thankfully supported by the investments Freedom Mortgage has made in supporting technology and people.

If you are aware of indicators like employment and interest rates, and stay in touch with the markets and investors, then you know you're moving in a rhythm that supports the elements of production tied to the elements of the cycle so that you're deeply living in tomorrow, Stan argues:

"That perspective helps you deal with outsized, black swan type events like COVID-19 or having a shotgun shoved in my face. There are always surprises and the unexpected in life; it's part of learning to live outside of our perceived comfort zones. In any business decision, you want to try and look beyond today's challenges. We're talking about not just tomorrow the next day, but about a tomorrow far, far into the future. As far as four or five or six years and more."

Being sensitive to what's happening in the world around you is perhaps the key talent that owners and managers must possess in order to be successful. We must watch carefully the timelines in which events are happening, Stan asserts, because it is essential to get a good understanding across a broad spectrum of ideas. Whether it's regulatory, governmental, economic, technological, judicial, or whatever the category is, having an understanding of how those dominoes line up is essential.

What are the elements that can make them fall, and in what sequence do we expect them to fall? This thinking, this pattern of behavior, this living in tomorrow, becomes ultimately the most critical of events for a strategist. Because a strategist is not someone who says "I think this, go do that," and that makes them successful. Rather, it is more like, "I think this because my understanding of this."

One fascinating aspect of Stan's approach to management is his focus on the team and the need to communicate ideas and goals in a way that members of the team can understand and get behind. "One of the great offshoots of being an informed strategist and having strategies evolve that are well-thought out and are readily supported is that it's easier to get buy-in from your team, your lenders, and your business partners," Stan said in one of our first interviews.

I've often said the right ten people can do anything they set their minds to accomplish. However, the more seasoned, the more accomplished those ten people are, the more difficult it is to convince them that buy-in is not just the right thing to do, it's the enlightened thing for them to do. It's right not only for you and for the organization, but for themselves. As the manager, your strategy has to make your implementation and acceptance of that direction in the best interest of the enlightened people that you ask to help you achieve it. Your activities have to move in the enlightened person's best interest of what, in effect, become your disciples on the execution of this plan. They need to take this plan, own it and carry it with energy and enthusiasm out to the masses. They must make it a way of life, and a way to do things.

Stan has argued over the years that success in business is all about living in tomorrow and bringing people with you. You have to have your ideas well aligned with the facts and well supported. The story you tell about the tomorrow you see must be a vision that others can see, and others will buy into, and others will accept as their enlightened self-interest view of tomorrow. From the earliest days of Freedom Mortgage in the 1990s, Stan has always managed to lead his team by example, by asking many, many questions, but by providing a clear vision of where Freedom Mortgage needs to go as it has become one of the largest private companies in the United States.

> The great thing about people and organizations is that they need to be prepared to sacrifice today, or the short run, in order to achieve a greater tomorrow. The shared vision of where they want to go becomes who they are and part of the life that they live. They adopt and accept and embellish and promote the shared strategy and vision. All because you've done the hard work of thinking about what that vision needs to be. That's really what seeing around corners is all about. It's about living in tomorrow, and then getting those around you to buy into that vision along with you.

The Next Housing Crisis

By the start of 2022, the mortgage industry had just completed the second of two extraordinary years, but the warning signs of a change in monetary policy were growing. Profit per loan in 2021 was less than half the record 1.5 percent realized in 2020, according to the

MBA survey, mostly the last nine months of the year.[34] And it also became clear that policymakers at the Fed and in Congress had done a little too much in response to COVID-19, in terms of both dropping interest rates and fiscal spending.

In February 2021, former Treasury secretary Lawrence Summers warned that President Biden's stimulus package was far too large and would lead to runaway inflation. Many observers "thought the Federal Reserve would be willing to raise interest rates to head off any inflationary problem," wrote *Wall Street Journal* columnist James McIntosh in June 2022. "My faith was misplaced, and it took me until June to realize my mistake. The Fed waited another nine months to act."[35]

Even though the Fed had begun to talk about a policy change in March 2022, there was little action. FOMC had acquired almost $3 trillion in MBSs as part of the "go big" response to COVID-19. Another $2 trillion in cash had been absorbed from banks and money market funds that were endangered by the near-zero interest rates that had prevailed from March 2020. All told, the FOMC owned over $9 trillion in securities, making the central bank more involved in financial markets and housing than ever before. Alex Pollock, former head of the Federal Home Loan Bank of Chicago and the father of the bank's mortgage loan purchase program, warned that the Fed had discarded past caution and is now the chief factor influencing housing. He put the situation in perspective in *Housing Finance International*:[36]

---

34   Mortgage Bankers Association, "Quarterly Mortgage Bankers Performance Report: Q1 2021."

35   James Mackintosh, "Larry Summers Nailed Inflation. But Is He Right on What Comes Next?" *Wall Street Journal*, June 27, 2022, https://www.wsj.com/articles/larry-summers-nailed-inflation-but-is-he-right-on-what-comes-next-11656343688.

36   Alex J. Pollock, "The Government Triangle at the Heart of U.S. Housing Finance," Housing Financial International, June 29 2022, https://www.alexjpollock.com/work-and-media/ewn3jzj64ookl7iiqnd1431er5lg1j.

"The US central bank's great twenty-first-century monetization of residential mortgages, with $2.7 trillion of mortgage securities on the books of the Federal Reserve, is a fundamental expansion of the role of the government in the American housing finance system… As the Federal Reserve now moves to address the inflation, interest rates on the standard American thirty-year fixed rate mortgage have gone from their suppressed level of 3 percent in 2021 to about 5½ percent in May 2022. Although historically speaking, that is still rather low, it will make many houses unaffordable for those who need a mortgage loan to buy. The interest expense for the same-sized mortgage for the same-priced house has increased by about 80 percent. How much higher might mortgage interest rates go? With higher mortgage rates, how quickly will the runaway house price inflation end? Will that be followed by a fall in US house prices from their current bubble heights? We are waiting to see."

Stan would probably say that the Fed has always been, indirectly, the chief influence on housing going back to the Volcker era. But now the central bank became far more overt and some might say reckless in pursuing the legal mandate of full employment and price stability. In June 2022, as the FOMC explained why rising interest rates and the related decline of value of its securities portfolio were not a cause for concern, the money markets, banks, funds, and independent mortgage banks were facing mounting financial and operational problems because of the market volatility created by the Fed actions. Benchmarks like the ten-year Treasury note now move double digits in yield on a daily basis, a reality that is reflected in the higher cost of hedging interest rate risk charged by dealers. The simpler days of the 1990s, when Stan first began to use employment and inflation as the guides for his business, have been replaced by a more volatile and less certain world where central banks are directly intervening in the markets.

Despite the gigantic changes underway in the mortgage market, Stan was relatively calm as smaller firms, such as First Guaranty and Sprott, were forced to close their doors in the first six months of 2022. By that December, Ginnie Mae was forced to seize the servicing asset from Reverse Mortgage Investment Trust, which filed bankruptcy at the end of November. This was the first seizure of a Ginnie Mae MSR since Taylor Bean & Whittaker in 2009 and caused a chill in the market for financing government assets. Reverse Mortgage ultimately cost the Treasury billions of dollars in expenses. And yet, Stan saw these tribulations as inevitable as he described his current view for how the economy and the mortgage market were going to evolve through the end of the decade.

"Most people see a recession forming in the near term, which will be followed by an eventual fall in interest rates and another upward surge in lending volumes and home purchases," Stan described in 2023. "We also anticipate an easing of credit for home buyers on the heels of the interest rate cut and lenders will rebuild their infrastructure to accommodate rising volumes. And there will be a lot of pressure to widen the credit box as demand for housing is eventually satisfied."

In the middle of 2022, calls for credit expansion were already very clear. The Biden administration made a cut in insurance premiums for FHA loans. And the regulator for Fannie Mae and Freddie Mac was also seeking to widen the box for low-income borrowers, part of a Washington ritual involving the Housing Industrial Complex. Homeownership was around 65 percent in the summer of 2022, according to the St. Louis Fed, well below the 70 percent prior to the 2008 maxi housing correction.[37] Many analysts would argue that pushing homeownership above current levels would eventually cause

---

37   FRED, "Homeownership Rate in the United States," updated August 2, 2023, accessed September 2023, https://fred.stlouisfed.org/series/RHORUSQ156N.

another credit crisis, but historically, the politics of homeownership is too powerful for rational arguments to prevail. This time, however, Stan sees a change in homeownership and the market for housing.

"It's been a long time since people saw credit expansion in mortgages. With homeownership approaching 66 percent, my view is that this level is about right to avoid problems down the road," Stan relates. "At the same time, I am worried about homeownership going forward. More of the new housing stock that is coming online is for single-family rentals than for purchase. The single-family rental business will continue to grow. Existing inventory was being bought up by Wall Street investment houses through 2022, but has slowed since."

Stan believes that homeownership is going to be under siege in the future in economic terms:

"We'll look more and more like Europe for lower income families, but we'll still preserve the notion of the American dream for political purposes. But owning a home will require decisions by policymakers in Washington, whether it's the Fed or Congress or a regulatory agency. Trying to support homeownership is very powerful politically, but in a market with investors buying homes for rental and too few new homes be created for purchase, home prices will remain high."

Affordability has been largely destroyed by the sharp home price appreciation courtesy of the Federal Reserve; thus, there is a great temptation for politicians to get involved. The fact that home prices rose because of COVID-19 and the subsequent inflation does not alter the desire of elected officials to be helpful, often in partnership with members of the housing industry. As we've discussed earlier in this book, Stan witnessed the dawn of the world of residential mortgage finance in the late 1980s as the S&L industry evaporated in a wave of interest rate and credit risk that took a decade to clean up.

Again, we need to recall that Paul Volcker hindered a lot of home builders and lenders when he raised interest rates to fight inflation in the late 1970s. In the 1990s, as Stan witnessed, banks like Norwest and Citibank were the buyers of excess loan production from small mortgage banks. By the 2000s, the GSEs Fannie Mae and Freddie Mac were the buyers of first resort, the ready money that provided the liquidity in the market for private, subprime mortgages until the music stopped and investors stepped back.

In the period since 2008, the mortgage market has evolved from a bank-centric model to a model with nonbank mortgage firms at the center, financed largely in the bond market and on bank balance sheets. Commercial banks and credit unions still own about a quarter of all residential loans, but banks are as much buyers as lenders in today's market. We see large nonbank finance companies making and selling the mortgage loans but retaining the servicing asset. These nonbank companies obtain financing from banks and in the bond market, but they are entirely dependent upon these primary sources for working capital. What differentiates the larger mortgage banks from the commercial banks? The former are far more efficient operationally and better able to manage liquidity and business risk, while commercial banks are designed to lend on collateral and absorb credit risk.

The mortgage market reset that Stan Middleman sees in the distance as the 2020s ends will test the skill of all of the players in the mortgage sector, banks, and nonbanks alike. While the underlying mortgages are insured by the US Treasury, the credit and interest rate risk contained in the $13 trillion in residential mortgages is considerable. Indeed, one point that Stan has come back to on more than one occasion is that 2020 when the Fed began its largest round of quantitive easing (QE) is likely to be the floor of the reset that comes between now and say 2027. As Stan likes to say, "misery on the 8s" in reference to a possible housing market reset in 2028.

Historically, corrections in home prices in the 1980s and 2000s came about because the supply of housing eventually caught up with demand, and then home prices fell back to the peak of the previous cycle. This is essentially how Stan would describe the past couple of cycles in housing. Prior to the 1980s, the US mortgage market was small and dominated by state-chartered banks and thrifts, which mostly made or purchased loans and kept them. The large national banks and GSEs really did not play in housing in a serious way in terms of buying loans for portfolio until the 1990s, as we detailed earlier. But in the 2020s, the market dynamic changed significantly because of (1) inflation and (2) the growing presence of Wall Street investors in the residential housing market, a market that traditionally was the exclusive province of consumers. As a result, the way the market expands and eventually corrects downward is likely to be very different.

"When we finally see interest rates fall in 2024 or after, the pressure on politicians to be helpful will be intense, but politically good intentions to support homeownership will become problematic," Stan relates.

Using public policy to push homeownership up will ultimately result in credit problems just as it did in 2008. Think of every loan made from say 2022 through to the major correction in five or six years as being a potential credit problem. All of those loans will be underwater in a correction and many will belong to low-income families that perhaps should not have bought a home—especially near the top of the home price cycle. Using government policy to put low-income families into a house that is already overvalued due to a lack of homebuilding is a recipe for disaster.

"Ultimately the lack of supply and the runup in the price of homes during the 2020s, combined with a deterioration in credit and continued increase in rentals will boost building, and ultimately satiate demand for homes at least partially," Stan continues. "Low interest rates and massively wider credit funnels fueled by political considerations could lead the US to another massive housing correction. You may not see home building start to accelerate until the middle of the decade, but high prices will attract builders. We'll have a relatively short recession followed by a massive recovery and widening of credit standards, and a spike in housing values, then we'll see a major home price correction."

Stan believes that when the economy eventually stumbles, the Fed will shift its focus back to employment from fighting inflation. We'll have some event that hurts the economy and causes the political narrative to shift away from inflation and toward preventing a deep recession, and then the housing market will experience one last hurrah before a major home price correction occurs.

"When the Fed finally begins to reduce interest rates, first we are going to see home prices rise and full employment," Stan predicts. "Home building will surge to meet pent-up demand, and investors will start to acquire existing homes and commercial properties for conversions. But then we are going to go over that hill and see a steep correction in asset values, particularly in residential housing."

Stan believes that interest rates could remain elevated for several years, meaning that loan origination volumes will be suppressed for several years compared with 2020 and 2021. This means that the mortgage industry will consolidate massively. Only firms with large servicing books will survive, and even some of the largest nonbank lenders will eat into the value of their assets trying to preserve a lending business that may never come back. And banks dealing with the new Basel III bank capital rules proposed in 2023, which increase the amount of capital banks must hold to back their assets, will also be sellers of residential mortgage assets, Stan believes.

"Think about mortgages and what residential mortgages look like as an industry," Stan argues.

> Who do you think about when you mention bonds? PIMCO, right? Who do you think about when you think about mutual funds and 401(k)s? Black Rock and Vanguard. So why would mortgages not also be dominated by one or more large nonbank players that achieve sufficient size and market share? You are going to see significant reductions in the market share and servicing portfolios of the banks due to Basel. Several large nonbanks lenders will consolidate the industry in a way that was not possible previously. As the mortgage industry does $2 trillion in production per year at higher interest rates, the value of the older production from 2020–2021 will increase. Newer production and servicing assets with higher coupons will get crushed in the next home price correction.

Seeing Around Corners

As Freedom Mortgage enters its fourth decade, the changes in the market for residential mortgages are profound. Stan has witnessed a market that began the 1990s with few banks participating directly in the mortgage market, followed by a period when the banks essentially took over the market. After 2008, the commercial banks exited the market for making loans to low-income families, leaving the world of low FICO borrowers to nonbank lenders such as Freedom Mortgage. The collapse of Fannie Mae and Freddie Mac into government conservatorship in September 2008 led to further shrinkage of the role of the GSEs in the mortgage market, further increasing the role of nonbanks in the mortgage market. But it is important to remember that nonbanks like insurers and thrifts were the first mortgage lenders.

Stan and other operators in the industry have seen the large banks and GSEs like Fannie Mae and Freddie Mac take over the mortgage market in the late 1990s and 2000s, only to be crushed in the massive market correction of 2008. In the market correction of 2008, roughly half of the large banks in the United States failed, and two of the three GSEs ended up under government conservatorship. As in the early 1990s, Citibank was again crippled by subprime mortgage exposures in 2008. Banks such as J.P. Morgan Chase completely exited the world of government lending, contributing to the sharp increase in market share for nonbanks over the next decade.

As 2023 came to a close, federal bank regulators planned further increases in capital requirements for banks, new levies that will make mortgage lending to the bottom half of Americans based upon income completely unattractive for banks. And Fannie Mae, Freddie Mac, and the Federal Home Loan Banks remain focused on catering to banks even as nonbanks are closing in on 75 percent market share in residential mortgages.

The prospect of higher capital requirements for banks via the latest Basel capital proposal is a big negative for the US housing sector. The new rule will raise capital requirements for large banks by some 20 percent and increase the risk weighting for residential mortgage family loans to prohibitive levels. The proposal is so radical that it has caused a diverse coalition of groups in the housing industry to come together to defeat the new Basel proposal. "This unnecessary proposal will increase borrowing costs and reduce credit availability for the very consumers and borrowers this administration ostensibly seeks to assist," said MBA president and CEO Bob Broeksmit.[38]

Even as the Fed and other central banks are using higher interest rates to combat inflation, the impact on mortgage markets that have grown accustomed to low interest rates over the past decade is harsh and increasingly problematic. While loan delinquency in residential mortgages remained relatively muted in the United States in 2023, in the United Kingdom, where most mortgages are floating rate, the result has been a disaster.

"It's a bloodbath, that's the way I'd like to describe it," says John, a father of two struggling with the ever-increasing interest rate on his home loan. He is one of the 1.4 million people in the United Kingdom on a variable rate residential mortgage, who watched their monthly payments soar after the Bank of England raised the key base interest rate to a fifteen-year high, the *Guardian* reported.[39]

The combination of central banks trying to fight inflation and prudential regulators seeking to reduce or limit risk to banks and government agencies, such as Fannie Mae, Freddie Mac, and Ginnie Mae, raises the specter of a reduction in support for housing in Washington—precisely at the time it is needed the most. During the first half of 2023, for example, Fannie Mae and Freddie Mac imposed punitive pricing on conventional lenders as punishment for not supporting the political objectives of the Biden administration. At the

---

38   MBA Newslink, "Banking Agencies Issue MBA-Opposed Proposed Changes to Bank Capital Requirements," July 28, 2023, https://newslink.mba.org/mba-news-links/2023/july/mba-newslink-friday-july-28-2023/mba-opposes-proposed-rulemak-ing-implementing-basel-iii-endgame-and-making-changes-to-capital-requirements-for-banks/.

39   Jess Clark, "'It's a Bloodbath': The UK Homeowners on Variable Rate Mortgages," *The Guardian,* August 3, 2023, https://www.theguardian.com/money/2023/aug/03/its-a-bloodbath-the-uk-homeowners-on-variable-mortgages-fearing-another-rate-rise.

same time, the GSEs began to increase requirements for loan review prior to close and loan repurchase demands on nonbank lenders, as though they wanted to get their money before the lenders failed.

"In speaking to lenders, the feedback was consistent," wrote former MBA CEO David Stevens in April 2023. "They believe that both GSEs changed their sampling methodology for quality control review earlier this year with specific focus on nonbank originators. Why would the GSEs focus on IMBs? It's rumored that this more aggressive posture is because they are concerned about potential failures of some of their customers during these tough times and therefore, they would lose their counterparty to warranty defects on loans should they go to default."[40]

Stevens notes that even as nonbank lenders have been losing money because of higher interest rates in 2023, the GSEs are reporting record profits. Any pretense of the GSEs supporting housing afford-ability and market stability, two of the key rationales for the creation of Fannie Mae ninety years ago, is long gone in Washington. The GSEs may never leave government control, but they behave more and more like predatory private corporations than public agencies. Moreover, the GSEs refuse to support market liquidity by repackag-ing seasoned loans from community banks and loans with minor defects, a role they once played to the benefit of the housing market and consumers alike.

As this book was being finalized, the FDIC validated all of the conversations we have had with Stan about the financial and other dangers facing conventional lenders because of loan putbacks and other types of claims from the GSEs—and other government

---

40   David Stevens, "Opinion: The GSEs Are Targeting IMBs on Buybacks," Hous-ingWire, accessed September 2023, https://www.housingwire.com/articles/opinion-the-gses-are-targeting-imbs-on-buybacks/.

agencies. Fifteen years after Washington Mutual's failure, the FDIC sued CTX Mortgage Company, which was acquired by the Pulte-Group in 2009, for selling "defective loans" funded by Washington Mutual into residential mortgage-backed securities (RMBS) trusts. In mortgage lending, the potential liability from a loan can last years or even decades, one reason why Stan and his team have always been very careful about what loans they make and to whom they sell those loans.

Whenever the world of credit is in transition, Stan emphasizes sensitivity and living in today. In 2022, Freedom Mortgage began to consciously slow their origination of conventional loans in order to moderate any economic, credit, or manufacturing risk from these loans. It took the markets most of 2022 to notice that the Fed was raising interest rates and for loan volumes to slow, especially in private-label loans. And strong home prices provided at least the appearance of a market with little concern about credit risk. Yet, the slowdown in private lending in the first half of 2023 proves yet again that interest rates matter.

The "fringe" financial products that exist in good times with low interest rates can quickly disappear when funding costs climb, and the threat of default risk comes back into focus after a period of exuberance. One key example of this is the market for private-label mortgages, which are loans without a guaranty on credit loss. Once interest rates rise, Stan notes, these markets literally start to disappear.

During 2023, the market for private-label mortgages essentially went to zero as investors stepped back and waited for new loans with higher coupons to stabilize in price. Yet, the market for private-label loans has grown enormously, with larger, more expensive homes rising in price at twice the rate of lower-priced homes. Yet, with increased concerns about risks from all mortgage loans and securities, banks may no longer be willing to hold as much mortgage risk as in past years. This means that the health of the market for private mortgages will become more critical for affluent consumers and the economy and also an important indicator of overall market health.

"After the FOMC allows interest rates to fall in 2024 or even 2025, we will have a period of higher home prices and rising loan volumes," Stan argued in August 2023.

The credit box will expand and capacity will be increased. But once the uptick in the housing market runs its course over a couple of years, inflation will increase and the Fed will again be forced to step on the brakes. We'll see the private market retreat again as it did in 2023. There's really no private-label securitization business today. And when the market corrects in 2027 or 2028, we'll take home prices back down perhaps to 2020 levels.

When you come to appreciate Stan's relatively simple yet nuanced view of the housing market, his prognostications about the future take on great importance—especially when we recall how well that Stan anticipated and managed through the 2008 financial crisis. By fading away from the conventional market and focusing instead on government lending, Stan and his team not only survived but also prospered, growing Freedom Mortgage's business organically and through acquisitions when other firms were in retreat.

One important investment that Stan made in 2023 was acquiring a stake in the Philadelphia Phillies baseball team, fulfilling a lifelong dream of being directly involved in his favorite sport. Stan agreed in January 2023 to buy one-third of the Buck family's interest in the team. Stan's addition to the ownership group marks only the second time in more than forty years that the Phillies have added a new partner. The first came in 1994, when the Middleton family purchased 15 percent of the team.[41]

"As evidenced by the great success of Freedom Mortgage, Stan is driven to succeed," said John Middleton, managing partner of the Phillies. "I admire his passion, commitment and perseverance in building his business. Those qualities, and many more, make Stan an important addition to our ownership group."

But the key insight for the author is that Stan has always managed his business as a portfolio of assets and risks. Deciding what is in that portfolio, or not, may be among Stan's most important legacies. Deciding to sell the loan but retain the servicing asset, for example, is one of the key strategic choices that every mortgage lender must decide.

"The solution for the next housing crisis is looking a little shaky at present," Stan muses.

Three or four years from now, the private-label securitization market is where the next crisis will start. Banks will not be buyers of large private mortgage loans as they have in the past. When the bond market shuts down, these mortgages will be orphans. But even more problematic will be all of the unconventional single and multifamily properties and converted commercial buildings which will also be shut out of financing. How is this going to look? I don't know precisely, but it is the jumbo private mortgages and loans on unconventional properties that will change the most. The conventional mortgages that are written up in valuation over the next two or three or four years will be underwater in the next correction.

---

41   Scott Lauber, "A New Limited Partner Is Joining the Phillies' Ownership Group," *The Philadelphia Inquirer*, January 6, 2023, https://www.inquirer.com/phillies/phillies-ownership-new-limited-partner-middleman-20230606.html.

TURNING THE NEXT CORNER

Stan worries that the tendency of the GSEs to push up the value of home prices in a falling interest rate environment will result in significant liquidity risk for lenders when rates subsequently rise. He sees a lot of credit and liquidity issues approaching in the future, but then when interest rates fall, things will seem to be getting better in the near term. The next two to three years are going to lull people into a false sense of security, Stan argues, but he expects a significant correction in the housing market after the next down cycle by the Fed in terms of interest rates.

Over the course of this narrative, you should have gained a sense for Stan Middleman as an entrepreneur and a person. We have discussed how focus, discipline, and hard work can create enormous success. At the same time, we have talked about how unseen risks can spoil the best laid plans, even when the horizon seems to be clear of hazards. We have talked about how building a shared vision can help to surmount challenges, but being lucky doesn't hurt either. And being prepared to take advantage of good fortune is even better. Despite his somewhat dire predictions about the mortgage industry at the end of the decade of the 2020s, Stan remains very excited about the future, both for himself and for his family at Freedom Mortgage:

"I am pretty excited about where we are today as an organization. The best is yet to come. We are going to get better at what we do, and we are going to continue to grow our financial and human assets. There are so many opportunities being created even as the housing market heads for a long-term price reset at the end of the decade."

That, at the end of the day, is what seeing around corners is all about.

ABOUT THE SUBJECT

Stanley C. Middleman is the founder, president, and CEO of Freedom Mortgage, one of the largest and fastest-growing independent mortgage companies in the country. He is a nationally recognized business strategist, investor, and philanthropist with more than thirty years of experience in the mortgage banking industry. Since founding Freedom Mortgage in 1990, Stan has grown the company into one of the nation's largest nonbank mortgage lenders and servicers, as well as a top VA and FHA government-insured lender.

Stan is a much sought-after speaker, frequently addressing peers, housing industry veterans, government officials, business leaders, and students on a variety of topics, including entrepreneurship, leadership, customer service, and building communities through homeownership.

Additionally, Stan is an investor and Vice Chairman of the Philadelphia Phillies baseball team.

Stan is an active member of the MBA, where he serves on the MBA Board of Directors. He has also served on numerous advisory boards in the mortgage industry, including the MBA Residential Board of Governors, as well as Freddie Mac, Fannie Mae, and Ellie Mae. He is currently a member of the Housing Policy Executive

Council. Stan also serves on several nonprofit boards, including Philadelphia's Kimmel Center for the Performing Arts, the Philadelphia Art Museum, and the Children's Hospital of Philadelphia (CHOP) Foundation Board of Advisors.

Because of their deep commitment to giving back and helping those in need, Stan and his family made a personal donation to support the opening of CHOP's second hospital (in King of Prussia, Pennsylvania). The 250,000 square-foot facility is named the Middleman Family Pavilion.

He also established The Stanley C. Middleman Center for Innovation in Accounting at the Fox School of Business at Temple. As a Temple University alumnus, he founded the Stanley Middleman Center for Jewish Life—Rohr Chabad for students to reconnect with their heritage on campus.

At Freedom Mortgage, Stan encouraged the creation of Freedom Mortgage Cares to engage employees to support and volunteer within their local communities through annual campaigns focused on supporting food banks, veterans, and active military.

Freedom Mortgage ranked on the Inc. 5000 Honor Roll (2023) for the ninth time as one of the fastest-growing private companies in the country. The company proudly offers a vibrant work environment where all team members can thrive. Freedom Mortgage was honored for the fourth year in a row as a 2024 Top Workplace in the United States. In addition, in 2023, Freedom Mortgage was named as a Top Workplace in the Philadelphia region by the *Philadelphia Inquirer*, as a Top Workplace in Central Indiana by the *Indianapolis Star*, and as a Top Workplace in New Jersey by *The Star-Ledger*. In 2022, Freedom Mortgage was named a Best-in-Class Employer by Gallagher, and in 2021, the company was named one of *Newsweek*'s Most Loved Workplaces.

Stan is proud to lead Freedom Mortgage in partnering with Live Nation and sponsor an outdoor amphitheater and indoor theater complex in Camden, New Jersey, located across from Philadelphia, called the Freedom Mortgage Pavilion.

Stan has been honored with the following:

- 2023 Community Champion Award by MBA's Opens Doors Foundation
- 2023 One of 150 Most Influential Philadelphians by *Philadelphia Magazine*
- 2023 Legends of Lending Award by *Mortgage Banker Magazine*
- 2023 Industry Titans Award by *National Mortgage Professional Magazine*
- 2022 The Distinguished Career Award by the Mortgage Executive Roundtable
- 2022 An Impact 50 leader by City & State PA
- 2021 A Top CEO by *South Jersey Business Magazine*
- 2020 Fifth highest-rated CEO by Glassdoor for effectively leading his employees and the company during the COVID-19 pandemic
- 2020 Most Admired CEO by *Philadelphia Business Journal*
- 2019 Ernst & Young Entrepreneur of the Year Greater Philadelphia Award in the financial services category
- 2019 Individual Honoree of the Year by the American Cancer Society of Southern New Jersey
- 2019 Temple University Fox School of Business Corporate Award
- 2019 Fox School of Business Centennial Award
- 2018 HousingWire's prestigious Vanguard Award
- 2018 Liberty USO Chairman's Award in honor of his support of the military community within Pennsylvania and Southern New Jersey

ABOUT THE AUTHOR

Richard Christopher Whalen is an investment banker and author who lives in New York. He is chairman of Whalen Global Advisors LLC and focuses on the banking, mortgage finance, and fintech sectors. Christopher is a contributing editor at *National Mortgage News* and publishes *The Institutional Risk Analyst* newsletter.

Over the past three decades, Chris worked as an author, a financial professional, and a journalist in Washington, New York, and London. He has held positions in the House Republican Conference Committee, the Federal Reserve Bank of New York, Bear, Stearns & Co., Prudential Securities, Tangent Capital, and Carrington Mortgage Holdings. In 1993, Chris was the first journalist to report on the then-secret FOMC minutes concealed by Fed chairman Alan Greenspan.

Christopher holds a BA in history from Villanova University. He is the author of three books, including his most recent work *Ford Men: From Inspiration to Enterprise* (2017), a study of Ford Motor Co. and the Ford family, published by Laissez Faire Books. He is the author of *Inflated: How Money and Debt Built the American Dream* (2010), published by John Wiley & Sons and co-author of *Financial Stability: Fraud, Confidence & the Wealth of Nations*, also published by John Wiley & Sons.

WWW.RCWHALEN.COM